But Joy Comes in the Morning

Studies on Joy

Based on *He Still Moves Stones*

Max Lucado

General Editor

Contents

Introduction

"Weeping may remain for a night, but joy comes in the morning." (Ps. 30:5)

It may seem a bit strange that the psalmist included *weeping* and *joy* in the same sentence.

But this verse is a reminder of the peace that passes understanding—that, as followers of Christ, nothing can take from us the joy of the Lord.

No pain can deprive God's children of their hearts' contentment in trusting Him in every circumstance of life. Despite the weeping that comes in the night of sorrow or pain or shame or legalism. Despite the confusion that comes in the night of shame or legalism. Despite the despair that comes in the night of loneliness or separation.

For those who follow Jesus, joy comes in the morning of confident faith in a God who understands that despair, that confusion, those tears. It's the joy of Romans 8:35, 38: *"Can anything separate us from the love Christ has for us? Can troubles or problems or sufferings or hunger or nakedness or danger or violent death? ....I am sure that neither death, nor life, nor angels, nor ruling spirits, nothing now, nothing in the future, no powers, nothing above us, nothing below us, nor anything else in the whole world will ever be able to separate us from the love of God that is in Christ Jesus our Lord."*

Can there be a greater joy?

—*Max Lucado*

Not Guilty

"I also don't judge you guilty. You may go now, but don't sin anymore" (John 8:10-11, paraphrased).

If you have ever wondered how God reacts when you fail, frame these words and hang them on the wall. Read them. Ponder them. Drink from them. Stand below them and let them wash over your soul.

—Max Lucado

1. Think of a well-known person whose personal failure was covered by the media. How did he or she seem to cope with the shame of failure?

_____

_____

_____

_____

_____

_____

1

A Moment with Max

Max shares these insights with us in his book *He Still Moves Stones*.

Canyons of shame run deep. Gorges of never-ending guilt. Walls ribboned with the greens and grays of death. Unending echoes of screams. Put your hands over your ears. Splash water on your face. Stop looking over your shoulder. Try as you might to outrun yesterday's tragedies—their tentacles are longer than your hope.

Sometimes your shame is private. Pushed over the edge by an abusive spouse. Seduced by a compromising superior. No one else knows. But you know. And that's enough.

Sometimes it's public. Branded by a divorce you didn't want. Contaminated by a disease you never expected. Marked by a handicap you didn't create. And whether it's actually in their eyes or just in your imagination, you have to deal with it—you are marked: a divorcee, an invalid, an orphan, an AIDS patient.

Whether private or public, shame is always painful. And unless you deal with it, it is permanent. Unless you get help—the dawn will never come.

2. In our society, what things bring shame on a person?

_____

_____

_____

_____

_____

3. How have you seen the church respond to a person living with shame?

_____

_____

_____

_____

A Message from the Word

¹Jesus went to the Mount of Olives. ²But early in the morning he went back to the Temple, and all the people came to him, and he sat and taught them. ³The teachers of the law and the Pharisees brought a woman who had been caught in adultery. They forced her to stand before the people. ⁴They said to Jesus, "Teacher, this woman was caught having sexual relations with a man who is not her husband. ⁵The law of Moses commands that we stone to death every woman who does this. What do you say we should do?" ⁶They were asking this to trick Jesus so that they could have some charge against him.

But Jesus bent over and started writing on the ground with his finger. ⁷When they continued to ask Jesus their question, he raised up and said, "Anyone here who has never sinned can throw the first stone at her." ⁸Then Jesus bent over again and wrote on the ground.

⁹Those who heard Jesus began to leave one by one, first the older men and then the others. Jesus was left there alone with the woman standing before him. ¹⁰Jesus raised up again and asked her, "Woman, where are they? Has no one judged you guilty?"

¹¹She answered, "No one, sir."

Then Jesus said, "I also don't judge you guilty. You may go now, but don't sin anymore."

John 8:1-11

3

4. Why do you think the older people were the first to leave?

_____

_____

_____

_____

5. How do you reconcile the point Jesus was making with our need to confront sin in our society?

_____

_____

_____

6. Explain the difference between shame and guilt.

_____

_____

_____

_____

_____

More from the Word

¹⁵My eyes are always looking to the LORD for help.
    He will keep me from any traps.
¹⁶Turn to me and have mercy on me,
    because I am lonely and hurting.
¹⁷My troubles have grown larger;
    free me from my problems.
¹⁸Look at my suffering and troubles,
    and take away all my sins.
¹⁹Look at how many enemies I have!
    See how much they hate me!
²⁰Protect me and save me.
    I trust you, so do not let me be disgraced.
²¹My hope is in you,
    so may goodness and honesty guard me.

Psalm 25:15-21

7. What does it mean to be "put to shame"?

_____

_____

_____

_____

4

8. How would you outline the steps of finding healing from shame?

_____

_____

_____

_____

_____

9. How can we find comfort when we are dealing with shame in our lives?

_____

_____

_____

5

_____

_____

_____

My Reflections

Take him with you to your canyon of shame. Invite Christ to journey with you. Let him stand beside you as you retell the events of the darkest nights of your soul.

And then listen. Listen carefully. He's speaking.

"I don't judge you guilty."

And watch. Watch carefully. He's writing. He's leaving a message. Not in the sand, but on a cross.

Not with his hand, but with his blood.

His message has two words: Not guilty.

—Max

Journal

In what area of my life do I need to experience healing from shame?

For Further Study

To study more about shame, read Genesis 2:25; Job 10:15; Psalm 25:1-3; Proverbs 3:35; Proverbs 13:5; Proverbs 14:35; Proverbs 18:3; Romans 1:24-27.

Additional Questions

10. In what unhealthy ways do some people cope with shame?

_____

_____

_____

_____

_____

_____

_____

11. What steps can we take to help people deal with the shame they feel?

_____

_____

_____

_____

_____

_____

12. How can we tell the difference between feeling convicted of sin and feeling needlessly shamed?

_____

_____

_____

_____

_____

Additional Thoughts

_____

_____

_____

_____

_____

_____

_____

_____

_____

_____

_____

_____

9

A Family Affair

Tar-baby relationships—stuck together but falling apart.

It's like a crammed and jammed elevator. People thrust together by chance on a short journey, saying as little as possible. The only difference is you'll eventually get off the elevator and never see these folks again—not so with the difficult relative. Family reunions, Christmas, Thanksgiving, weddings, funerals—they'll be there.

Does Jesus have anything to say about dealing with difficult relatives? Is there an example of Jesus bringing peace to a painful family? Yes, there is.

His own. —Max Lucado

1. What circumstances or situations make family gatherings stressful?

_____

_____

_____

11

A Moment with Max

Max shares these insights with us in his book *He Still Moves Stones*.

It may surprise you to know that Jesus had a difficult family. It may surprise you to know that Jesus had a family at all! You may not be aware that Jesus had brothers and sisters. He did. Quoting Jesus' hometown critics, Mark wrote, "Isn't this [Jesus] the carpenter? Isn't this Mary's son and the brother of James, Joseph, Judas, and Simon? Aren't his sisters here with us?" (Mark 6:3).

And it may surprise you to know that his family was less than perfect. They were. If your family doesn't appreciate you, take heart, neither did Jesus'.

It's worth noting that he didn't try to control his family's behavior, nor did he let their behavior control his. He didn't demand that they agree with him. He didn't sulk when they insulted him. He didn't make it his mission to try to please them.

When Jesus' brothers didn't share his convictions, he didn't try to force them. He recognized that his spiritual family could provide what his physical family didn't. If Jesus himself couldn't force his family to share his convictions, what makes you think you can force yours?

12

2. What aspect of everyday family life is it most difficult for you to imagine Jesus experiencing? Why?

_____

_____

_____

_____

_____

3. How can having different convictions than members of your family cause strife and tension?

_____

_____

_____

_____

A Message from the Word

²⁰Then Jesus went home, but again a crowd gathered. There were so many people that Jesus and his followers could not eat. ²¹When his family heard this, they went to get him because they thought he was out of his mind. ²²But the teachers of the law from Jerusalem were saying, "Beelzebul is living inside him! He uses power from the ruler of demons to force demons out of people."

²³So Jesus called the people together and taught them with stories. He said, "Satan will not force himself out of people. ²⁴A kingdom that is divided cannot continue, ²⁵and a family that is divided cannot continue. ²⁶And if Satan is against himself and fights against his own people, he cannot continue; that is the end of Satan. ²⁷No one can enter a strong person's house and steal his things unless he first ties up the strong person. Then he can steal things from the house. ²⁸I tell you the truth, all sins that people do and all the things people say against God can be forgiven. ²⁹But anyone who speaks against the Holy Spirit will never be forgiven; he is guilty of a sin that continues forever."

³⁰Jesus said this because the teachers of the law said that he had an evil spirit inside him.

13

³¹Then Jesus' mother and brothers arrived. Standing outside, they sent someone in to tell him to come out. ³²Many people were sitting around Jesus, and they said to him, "Your mother and brothers are waiting for you outside."

³³Jesus asked, "Who are my mother and my brothers?" ³⁴Then he looked at those sitting around him and said, "Here are my mother and my brothers! ³⁵My true brother and sister and mother are those who do what God wants."

Mark 3:20–35

4. How do you think you would have reacted in this situation if you had been Jesus' brother or sister?

_____

_____

_____

_____

_____

5. In what ways have Christian friends become like family members to you?

_____

_____

_____

_____

_____

6. List several reasons why family relationships can be so challenging.

_____

_____

_____

_____

More from the Word

25"The older son was in the field, and as he came closer to the house, he heard the sound of music and dancing. 26So he called to one of the servants and asked what all this meant. 27The servant said, 'Your brother has come back, and your father killed the fat calf, because your brother came home safely.' 28The older son was angry and would not go in to the feast. So his father went out and begged him to come in. 29But the older son said to his father, 'I have served you like a slave for many years and have always obeyed your commands. But you never gave me even a young goat to have at a feast with my friends. 30But your other son, who wasted all your money on prostitutes, comes home, and you kill the fat calf for him!' 31The father said to him, 'Son, you are always with me, and all that I have is yours. 32We had to celebrate and be happy because your brother was dead, but now he is alive. He was lost, but now he is found.' "

Luke 15:25-32

7. If you had been in the older brother's position, how do you image you would have felt?

_____

_____

_____

_____

8. If you had been in the father's position, how do you think you might have dealt with your sons?

_____

_____

_____

_____

9. How can jealousy divide and destroy families?

15

_____

_____

_____

_____

My Reflections

I can't assure you that your family will ever give you the blessing you seek, but I know God will. Let God give you what your family doesn't. If your earthly father doesn't affirm you, then let your heavenly Father take his place.

He has provided for your needs (Matt. 6:25–34). He has protected you from harm (Ps. 139:5). He has adopted you (Eph. 1:5). And he has given you his name (1 John 3:1).

God has proven himself as a faithful father. Now it falls to us to be trusting children. Let God give you what your family doesn't. Let him fill the void others have left. Rely upon him for your affirmation and encouragement. Look at Paul's words: "You are God's child, and God will give you the blessing he promised, because you are his child" (Gal. 4:7).

—Max

Journal

How can I look to God to fulfill the needs that my family has not met in my life?

_____

_____

_____

_____

_____

_____

_____

_____

_____

_____

_____

For Further Study

To study more about family relationships, read Proverbs 11:29;
Proverbs 15:27; Proverbs 31:10-15; Acts 16:33-34; Ephes. 5:21-6:4;
Col. 3:18-21; 1 Tim. 3:1-5; 1 Tim. 5:4.

Additional Questions

10. List several things we expect to receive from our families.

_____

_____

_____

_____

_____

_____

11. How are our expectations different with friends than with family members?

_____

_____

_____

_____

_____

_____

12. Describe what you believe is your responsibility to your family.

_____

_____

_____

_____

_____

_____

Additional Thoughts

_____

_____ 19

_____

_____

_____

_____

_____

_____

_____

_____

_____

_____

_____

Sour Milk

Sweet milk turns sour from being too warm too long.

Sweet dispositions turn sour for the same reason. Let aggravation stew without a period of cooling down, and the result? A bad, bitter, clabberish attitude.

—Max Lucado

21

1. What kinds of attitudes could be associated with sour milk?

_____

_____

_____

_____

_____

_____

_____

A Moment with Max

Max shares these insights with us in his book *He Still Moves Stones*.

This chapter of Luke describes the step-by-step process of the sweet becoming sour.

It's the story of Martha. A dear soul given to hospitality and organization. More frugal than frivolous, more practical than pensive. Ask her to choose between a book and a broom, and she'll take the broom.

Mary, however, will take the book. Mary is Martha's sister. Same parents, different priorities. Martha has things to do. Mary has thoughts to think.

Apparently Martha worried too much, too. So much so that she started bossing God around. Worry will do that to you. It makes you forget who's in charge.

What makes this case interesting, however, is that Martha is worried about something good. She's having Jesus over for dinner. She's literally serving God. Her aim was to please Jesus. But, as she began to work for him her work became more important than her Lord. What began as a way to serve Jesus, slowly and subtly became a way to serve self.

One look at the flour-covered scowl will tell you that. "That Mary. Here I am alone in the kitchen while she's out there."

Oh boy. She's miffed. Look at her glaring over her shoulder through the doorway. That's Mary she's staring at. The one seated on the floor, listening to Jesus. "Lord, don't you care that my sister has left me alone to do all the work? Tell her to help me" (Luke 10:40).

It's easy to forget who is the servant and who is to be served.

Satan knows that. This tool of distortion is one of Satan's slyest. Note: He didn't take Martha out of the kitchen; he took away her purpose in the kitchen. He won't take you away from your ministry; he'll disillusion you in your ministry.

2. Describe someone you know who became disillusioned with ministry.

_____

_____

_____

3. How can we keep Satan from robbing us of our joy in our service to God?

_____

_____

A Message from the Word

[5]So put all evil things out of your life: sexual sinning, doing evil, letting evil thoughts control you, wanting things that are evil, and greed. This is really serving a false god. [6]These things make God angry. [7]In your past, evil life you also did these things.

[8]But now also put these things out of your life: anger, bad temper, doing or saying things to hurt others, and using evil words when you talk. [9]Do not lie to each other. You have left your old sinful life and the things you did before. [10]You have begun to live the new life, in which you are being made new and are becoming like the One who made you. This new life brings you the true knowledge of God. [11]In the new life there is no difference between Greeks and Jews, those who are circumcised and those who are not circumcised, or people who are foreigners, or Scythians. There is no difference between slaves and free people. But Christ is in all believers, and Christ is all that is important.

[12]God has chosen you and made you his holy people. He loves you. So always do these things: Show mercy to others, be kind, humble, gentle, and patient. [13]Get along with each other, and forgive each other. If someone does wrong to you, forgive that person because the Lord forgave you. [14]Do all these things; but most important, love each other. Love is what holds you all together in perfect unity. [15]Let the peace that Christ gives control your thinking, because you were all called together in one body to have peace. Always be thankful. [16]Let the teaching of Christ live in you richly. Use all wisdom to teach and instruct each other by singing psalms, hymns, and spiritual songs with thankfulness in your hearts to God. [17]Everything you do or say should be done to obey Jesus your Lord. And in all you do, give thanks to God the Father through Jesus.

Colossians 3:5-17

4. In what ways are our attitudes as evident as the clothes on our bodies?

5. What would you list as the three top attitudes Christians should exhibit?

_____

_____

_____

_____

6. What makes it so difficult to change a wrong attitude?

_____

_____

_____

_____

More from the Word

[38]While Jesus and his followers were traveling, Jesus went into a town. A woman named Martha let Jesus stay at her house. [39]Martha had a sister named Mary, who was sitting at Jesus' feet and listening to him teach. [40]But Martha was busy with all the work to be done. She went in and said, "Lord, don't you care that my sister has left me alone to do all the work? Tell her to help me."

[41]But the Lord answered her, "Martha, Martha, you are worried and upset about many things. [42]Only one thing is important. Mary has chosen the better thing, and it will never be taken away from her."

Luke 10:38-42

7. If you had been in Martha's shoes, how do you think you would have felt about doing all the work while Mary chatted with Jesus?

_____

_____

_____

_____

_____

8. How do you imagine Jesus's words changed Martha's attitude?

_____

_____

_____

_____

_____

9. How would you compare Martha's attitude to sour milk?

_____

_____

_____

_____

My Reflections

Guard your attitude.

What matters more than the type of service is the heart behind the service. A bad attitude spoils the gift we leave on the altar for God.

God has gifted you with talents. He has done the same to your neighbor. If you concern yourself with your neighbor's talents, you will neglect yours. But if you concern yourself with yours, you could inspire both.

—Max

Journal

What wrong attitudes do I need God's help to change?

For Further Study

To study more about attitudes, read Ephes. 4:21–5:2; Philip. 2:5–11; Philip. 4:8; Col. 3:12–17; Titus 1:15; Hebrews 4:12–13; 1 Peter 4:1–11.

Additional Questions

10. How would you define the word "attitude" to a child?

_____

_____

_____

_____

_____

_____

11. What practical steps can a person take to change a negative attitude?

_____

_____

_____

_____

_____

_____

12. If positive attitudes get us farther in life, why do we give in to negativity?

_____

_____

_____

_____

_____

_____

Additional Thoughts

_____

_____

_____

_____

_____

_____

_____

_____

_____

_____

_____

_____

_____

_____

Young at Heart?

A friend of the late American jurist Oliver Wendell Holmes asked him why he had taken up the study of Greek at the age of ninety-four. Holmes replied, "Well, my good sir, it's now or never."

When J. C. Penney was ninety-five years old, he affirmed, "My eyesight may be getting weaker, but my vision is increasing." —Max Lucado

31

1. Describe a person you know who has aged gracefully.

_____

_____

_____

_____

_____

_____

_____

A Moment with Max

Max shares these insights with us in his book *He Still Moves Stones*.

Let me be very clear with my point: Growing old can be dangerous. The trail is treacherous and the pitfalls are many. One is wise to be prepared. You know it's coming. It's not like God kept the process a secret. It's not like you are blazing a trail as you grow older. It's not as if no one has ever done it before. Look around you. You have ample opportunity to prepare and ample case studies to consider. If growing old catches you by surprise, don't blame God. He gave you plenty of warning. He also gave you plenty of advice.

"Whoever tries to keep his life safe will lose it, and the man who is prepared to lose his life will preserve it" (PHILLIPS).

"There are two ways to view life." Jesus is saying, "those who protect it or those who pursue it. The wisest are not the ones with the most years in their lives, but the most life in their years."

There is a rawness and a wonder to life. Pursue it. Hunt for it. Sell out to get it. Don't listen to the whines of those who have settled for a second-rate life and want you to do the same so they won't feel guilty. Your goal is not to live long; it's to live.

32

2. What is the difference between living long and *really* living?

_____

_____

_____

_____

3. Why do you think so many people fight the natural aging process?

_____

_____

_____

_____

A Message from the Word

[17]So I hated life. It made me sad to think that everything here on earth is useless, like chasing the wind. [18]I hated all the things I had worked for here on earth, because I must leave them to someone who will live after me. [19]Someone else will control everything for which I worked so hard here on earth, and I don't know if he will be wise or foolish. This is also useless. [20]So I became sad about all the hard work I had done here on earth. [21]People can work hard using all their wisdom, knowledge, and skill, but they will die, and other people will get the things for which they worked. They did not do the work, but they will get everything. This is also unfair and useless. [22]What do people get for all their work and struggling here on earth? [23]All of their lives their work is full of pain and sorrow, and even at night their minds don't rest. This is also useless.

[24]The best that people can do is eat, drink, and enjoy their work. I saw that even this comes from God, [25]because no one can eat or enjoy life without him.

Ecclesiastes 2:17-25

4. Describe in your own words the process of accepting one's own mortality.

_____

_____

_____

_____

_____

5. What are some fears people have about growing old?

_____

_____

_____

_____

_____

6. What criterion do you think we should use in looking back over a lifetime and evaluating it's worth?

_____

_____

_____

_____

_____

_____

More from the Word

34   ¹I have seen something else wrong here on earth that causes serious problems for people.

²God gives great wealth, riches, and honor to some people; they have everything they want. But God does not let them enjoy such things; a stranger enjoys them instead. This is useless and very wrong.

³A man might have a hundred children and live a long time, but what good is it if he can't enjoy the good God gives him or have a proper burial? I say a baby born dead is better off than he is.

⁴A baby born dead is useless. It returns to darkness without even a name.

⁵That baby never saw the sun and never knew anything, but it finds more rest than that man.

⁶Even if he lives two thousand years, he doesn't enjoy the good God gives him. Everyone is going to the same place.

Ecclesiastes 6:1-6

7. Describe a person (real or fictional) who has a good life but doesn't enjoy it to the fullest.

_____

_____

_____

_____

_____

_____

8. What are the "how to"s for enjoying the life God gives us?

_____

_____

_____

_____

9. Do you think old age gives you more or less ability to enjoy life?

_____

_____

_____

_____

My Reflections

Time slips. Days pass. Years fade. And life ends. And what we came to do must be done while there is time.

We would think it bizarre for a traveler not to be prepared for the end of the journey. We would pity the poor passenger who never read his itinerary. We'd be bewildered by someone who thought the purpose of the trip was the trip.

Others, however, are anticipating the destination. I hope you are. And I hope you'll be ready when you get home. For you, age is no enemy. Age is a mile-marker—a gentle reminder that home has never been so near.

—Max

Journal

What do I fear most about aging? Why?

For Further Study

To study more about aging, read 1 Chron. 29:26-28; Job 32:8-9; Proverbs 16:31; Proverbs 17:6; 1 Tim. 5:1-7; Titus 2:1-8; 1 Peter 5:5.

Additional Questions

10. What stage of life do you think is the best and which is the most challenging? Why?

_____

_____

_____

_____

_____

_____

11. What can we do when we feel discouraged about growing old?

_____

_____

_____

_____

_____

_____

12. In your opinion, what is the key to aging gracefully?

_____

_____

_____

_____

_____

Additional Thoughts

_____

_____

39

_____

_____

_____

_____

_____

_____

_____

_____

_____

_____

40

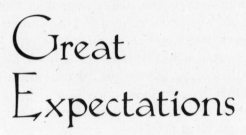

Great Expectations

When God doesn't do what we want, it's not easy. Never has been. Never will be. But faith is the conviction that God knows more than we do about this life and he will get us through it.

Remember, disappointment is caused by unmet expectations.

Disappointment is cured by revamped expectations.

—Max Lucado

41

1. When have you seen a person's expectations set them up for disappointment?

_____

_____

_____

_____

_____

_____

_____

A Moment with Max

Max shares these insights with us in his book *He Still Moves Stones*.

We're talking about what two friends of Jesus were feeling a couple of days after his death. Their world has tumbled in on them. It's obvious by the way they walk. Their feet shuffle, their heads hang, their shoulders droop. The seven miles from Jerusalem to Emmaus must feel like seventy.

As they walk a stranger comes up behind them. It is Jesus, but they don't recognize him. Disappointment will do that to you. It will blind you to the very presence of God. Discouragement turns our eyes inward. God would be walking next to us, but despair clouds our vision.

Despair does something else. Not only does it cloud our vision, it hardens our hearts. We get cynical. We get calloused. And when good news comes, we don't want to accept it for fear of being disappointed again. That's what happened to these two people.

The disciples had hoped Jesus would free Israel. They had hoped he'd kick out the Romans. They'd hoped Pilate would be out and Jesus would be in. But Pilate was still in, and Jesus was dead.

Unfulfilled expectations. God didn't do what they wanted him to.

They were good disciples. With good hearts and sincere prayers. They just had the wrong expectations.

42

2. How do most people deal with failed expectations?

_____

_____

_____

_____

3. What expectations should we have about what God will do for us?

_____

_____

_____

_____

A Message from the Word

[13]That same day two of Jesus' followers were going to a town named Emmaus, about seven miles from Jerusalem. [14]They were talking about everything that had happened. [15]While they were talking and discussing, Jesus himself came near and began walking with them, [16]but they were kept from recognizing him. [17]Then he said, "What are these things you are talking about while you walk?"

The two followers stopped, looking very sad. [18]The one named Cleopas answered, "Are you the only visitor in Jerusalem who does not know what just happened there?"

[19]Jesus said to them, "What are you talking about?"

They said, "About Jesus of Nazareth. He was a prophet who said and did many powerful things before God and all the people. [20]Our leaders and the leading priests handed him over to be sentenced to death, and they crucified him. [21]But we were hoping that he would free Israel. Besides this, it is now the third day since this happened. [22]And today some women among us amazed us. Early this morning they went to the tomb, [23]but they did not find his body there. They came and told us that they had seen a vision of angels who said that Jesus was alive! [24]So some of our group went to the tomb, too. They found it just as the women said, but they did not see Jesus."

Luke 24:13-24

43

4. If you had been one of these disciples, what emotions do you imagine you would have felt?

_____

_____

_____

_____

_____

5. If you had to guess the disciples' level of disappointment on a scale of 1–10 (10 being the most disappointment a person can bear), how would you rate it?

_____

_____

_____

_____

6. How can disappointment and despair hinder our faith?

_____

_____

_____

_____

More from the Word

²⁵Then Jesus said to them, "You are foolish and slow to believe everything the prophets said. ²⁶They said that the Christ must suffer these things before he enters his glory." ²⁷Then starting with what Moses and all the prophets had said about him, Jesus began to explain everything that had been written about himself in the Scriptures.

²⁸They came near the town of Emmaus, and Jesus acted as if he were going farther. ²⁹But they begged him, "Stay with us, because it is late; it is almost night." So he went in to stay with them.

³⁰When Jesus was at the table with them, he took some bread, gave thanks, divided it, and gave it to them. ³¹And then, they were allowed to recognize Jesus. But when they saw who he was, he disappeared. ³²They said to each other, "It felt like a fire burning in us when Jesus talked to us on the road and explained the Scriptures to us."

Luke 24:25-32

7. What tactic did Jesus use to help the disciples combat their disappointment?

_____

_____

8. How did Jesus change the disciples' expectations?

_____

_____

_____

_____

_____

_____

9. What kinds of expectations do we put on God that lead to disappointment?

_____

_____

45

_____

_____

_____

_____

My Reflections

The way to deal with discouragement? The cure for disappointment? Be reminded that you aren't the first person to weep. And you aren't the first person to be helped.

Next time you're disappointed, don't panic. Don't jump out. Don't give up. Just be patient and let God remind you he's still in control. It ain't over till it's over.

—Max

Journal

What improper expectations do I need to release to God?

_____

_____

_____

_____

_____

_____

_____

_____

_____

_____

_____

_____

_____

_____

_____

_____

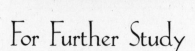

For Further Study

To study more about disappointment, read Psalm 25:1-3; Psalm 33:20-22; Psalm 42:10-11; Proverbs 13:12; Isaiah 40:27-31; Isaiah 49:23; Romans 5:1-5; 2 Cor. 4:7-12.

Additional Questions

10. What is the difference between discouragement and disappointment?

_____

_____

_____

_____

_____

_____

11. How do you pull yourself out of discouragement?

_____

_____

_____

_____

_____

_____

12. How do you cope with disappointment?

_____

_____

_____

_____

_____

_____

Additional Thoughts

_____

_____

_____

_____

_____

_____

_____

_____

_____

_____

_____

_____

_____

_____

50

Wrong Question, Right Answer

Sometimes God is so touched by what he sees that he gives us what we need and not simply that for which we ask.

We ask for little things like a long life and a healthy body and a good job. Grand requests from our perspective, but from God's it's like taking the moped when he offers the limo.

—Max Lucado

1. List some of the good gifts God has given you that you didn't expect.

_____

_____

_____

_____

_____

_____

_____

A Moment with Max

Max shares these insights with us in his book *He Still Moves Stones*.

The man couldn't walk. He couldn't stand. His limbs were bent and his body twisted. A waist-high world walked past as he sat and watched.

His friends tried to get some help for him. The four huddled over the paralytic and listened to the plan to climb to the top of the house, cut through the roof, and lower their friend down with their sashes. It was risky; it was unorthodox; it was intrusive; but it was their only chance.

Jesus was moved by the scene of faith—The friends want him to help their friend. But Jesus won't settle for a simple healing of the body—he wants to heal the soul. He leapfrogs the physical and deals with the spiritual. To heal the body is temporal; to heal the soul is eternal.

The request of the friends is valid, but timid. The expectations of the crowd are high, but not high enough. They expect Jesus to say, "I heal you." Instead he says, "I forgive you."

They want Jesus to give the man a new body so he can walk. Jesus gives grace so the man can live.

2. Describe the difference between spiritual brokenness and physical brokenness.

_____

_____

_____

_____

_____

3. Describe the difference between spiritual healing and physical healing.

_____

_____

_____

_____

A Message from the Word

[1]A few days later, when Jesus came back to Capernaum, the news spread that he was at home. [2]Many people gathered together so that there was no room in the house, not even outside the door. And Jesus was teaching them God's message. [3]Four people came, carrying a paralyzed man. [4]Since they could not get to Jesus because of the crowd, they dug a hole in the roof right above where he was speaking. When they got through, they lowered the mat with the paralyzed man on it. [5]When Jesus saw the faith of these people, he said to the paralyzed man, "Young man, your sins are forgiven."

[6]Some of the teachers of the law were sitting there, thinking to themselves, [7]"Why does this man say things like that? He is speaking as if he were God. Only God can forgive sins."

[8]Jesus knew immediately what these teachers of the law were thinking. So he said to them, "Why are you thinking these things? [9]Which is easier: to tell this paralyzed man, 'Your sins are forgiven,' or to tell him, 'Stand up. Take your mat and walk?' [10]But I will prove to you that the Son of Man has authority on earth to forgive sins." So Jesus said to the paralyzed man, [11]"I tell you, stand up, take your mat, and go home." [12]Immediately the paralyzed man stood up, took his mat, and walked out while everyone was watching him.

The people were amazed and praised God. They said, "We have never seen anything like this!"

Mark 2:1-12

53

4. Why do you think the teachers of the law were so offended by Jesus' words to the paralytic?

_____

_____

_____

_____

5. How do you imagine the paralytic felt when Jesus offered him forgiveness first without indicating whether he would heal his physical condition?

_____

_____

_____

_____

_____

6. What difference does it make in your life to know your sins are forgiven?

_____

_____

_____

_____

More from the Word

³⁷A sinful woman in the town learned that Jesus was eating at the Pharisee's house. So she brought an alabaster jar of perfume ³⁸and stood behind Jesus at his feet, crying. She began to wash his feet with her tears, and she dried them with her hair, kissing them many times and rubbing them with the perfume. ³⁹When the Pharisee who asked Jesus to come to his house saw this, he thought to himself, "If Jesus were a prophet, he would know that the woman touching him is a sinner!"

⁴⁰Jesus said to the Pharisee, "Simon, I have something to say to you."
Simon said, "Teacher, tell me."

⁴¹Jesus said, "Two people owed money to the same banker. One owed five hundred coins and the other owed fifty. ⁴²They had no money to pay what they owed, but the banker told both of them they did not have to pay him. Which person will love the banker more?"

⁴³Simon, the Pharisee, answered, "I think it would be the one who owed him the most money."

Jesus said to Simon, "You are right." ⁴⁴Then Jesus turned toward the woman and said to Simon, "Do you see this woman? When I came into your house, you gave me no water for my feet, but she washed my feet with her tears and dried them with her hair. ⁴⁵You gave me no kiss of greeting, but she has been kissing my feet since I came in. ⁴⁶You did not put oil on my head, but she poured perfume on my feet. ⁴⁷I tell you that her many sins are forgiven, so she showed great love. But the person who is forgiven only a little will love only a little."

⁴⁸Then Jesus said to her, "Your sins are forgiven."

⁴⁹The people sitting at the table began to say among themselves, "Who is this who even forgives sins?"

⁵⁰Jesus said to the woman, "Because you believed, you are saved from your sins. Go in peace."

Luke 7:37-50

7. If Jesus were here with us today, what do you think we would do to show our gratitude for his forgiveness?

_____

_____

_____

_____

_____

8. How does our awareness of our sin affect the depth of our gratitude?

55

_____

_____

_____

_____

_____

9. How do you demonstrate to God your gratitude for forgiveness of your sins?

_____

_____

_____

_____

My Reflections

By the way, he hasn't changed. What happened then happens today. When we take a step of faith, God sees. The same face that beamed at the paralytic beams at the alcoholic refusing the bottle. The same eyes that danced at the friends dance at the mom and dad who will do whatever it takes to get their child to Jesus. And the same lips that spoke to the man in Capernaum speak to the man in Detroit, to the woman in Belfast, to the child in Moscow . . . to any person anywhere who dares to come into the presence of God and ask for help.

And though we can't hear it here, the angels can hear him there. All of heaven must pause as another burst of love declares the only words that really matter: "Your sins are forgiven."

—Max

Journal

Write a praise letter to God, expressing your gratitude for forgiveness.

For Further Study

To study more about God's forgiveness, read Psalm 19:12-14; Psalm 32:1; Psalm 130:4-6; Matthew 6:12-15; Mark 3:28-29; Mark 11:25; Ephes. 1:7; Col. 1:9-14; Hebrews 9:22; 1 John 1:9.

Additional Questions

10. Describe someone in your life who has shown you forgiveness.

_____

_____

_____

_____

_____

_____

11. What does it feel like to forgive?

_____

_____

_____

_____

_____

12. What keeps some people from accepting God's offer of forgiveness?

_____

_____

_____

_____

_____

_____

Additional Thoughts

_____

_____ 59

_____

_____

_____

_____

_____

_____

_____

_____

_____

Laying Down the Law

You can't help the blind by turning up the light;

You can't help the deaf by turning up the music;

You can't change the inside by decorating the outside;

You can't grow fruit without seed;

You must be born again.

—Max Lucado

1. How do these statements relate to people who try to be righteous through obeying rules?

_____

_____

_____

_____

_____

_____

_____

A Moment with Max

Max shares these insights with us in his book *He Still Moves Stones*.

The meeting between Jesus and Nicodemus was more than an encounter between two religious figures. It was a collision between two philosophies. Two opposing views on salvation.

Nicodemus thought the person did the work: Jesus says God does the work. Nicodemus thought it was a tradeoff. Jesus says it is a gift. Nicodemus thought man's job was to earn it. Jesus says man's job is to accept it.

These two views encompass all views. All the world religions can be placed in one of two camps: legalism or grace. Humankind does it or God does it. Salvation as a wage based on deeds done—or salvation as a gift based on Christ's death.

A legalist believes the supreme force behind salvation is you. If you look right, speak right, and belong to the right segment of the right group, you will be saved. The brunt of responsibility doesn't lie within God—it lies within you.

Legalism doesn't need God. Legalism is the search for innocence—not forgiveness. It's a systematic process of defending self, explaining self, exalting self, and justifying self. Legalists are obsessed with self—not God.

62

2. What is your definition of legalism?

_____

_____

_____

_____

3. If our responsibility is to accept God's grace, how can we do that job well?

_____

_____

_____

_____

A Message from the Word

¹There was a man named Nicodemus who was one of the Pharisees and an important Jewish leader. ²One night Nicodemus came to Jesus and said, "Teacher, we know you are a teacher sent from God, because no one can do the miracles you do unless God is with him."

³Jesus answered, "I tell you the truth, unless one is born again, he cannot be in God's kingdom."

⁴Nicodemus said, "But if a person is already old, how can he be born again? He cannot enter his mother's body again. So how can a person be born a second time?"

⁵But Jesus answered, "I tell you the truth, unless one is born from water and the Spirit, he cannot enter God's kingdom. ⁶Human life comes from human parents, but spiritual life comes from the Spirit. ⁷Don't be surprised when I tell you, 'You must all be born again.' ⁸The wind blows where it wants to and you hear the sound of it, but you don't know where the wind comes from or where it is going. It is the same with every person who is born from the Spirit."

⁹Nicodemus asked, "How can this happen?"

¹⁰Jesus said, "You are an important teacher in Israel, and you don't understand these things?

¹⁶"God loved the world so much that he gave his one and only Son so that whoever believes in him may not be lost, but have eternal life. ¹⁷God did not send his Son into the world to judge the world guilty, but to save the world through him. ¹⁸People who believe in God's Son are not judged guilty. Those who do not believe have already been judged guilty, because they have not believed in God's one and only Son."

John 3:1-10; 16-18

63

4. Why do you imagine that the writer of this story bothered to mention that Nicodemus came to Jesus *at night*?

_____

_____

_____

_____

_____

5. How would you explain why Jesus' message of new life was confusing to a religious leader like Nicodemus?

_____

_____

_____

6. Since Nicodemus lived in a subculture where obeying the law made you righteous, how would Jesus' message change his life?

_____

_____

_____

More from the Word

²⁷So do we have a reason to brag about ourselves? No! And why not? It is the way of faith that stops all bragging, not the way of trying to obey the law. ²⁸A person is made right with God through faith, not through obeying the law. ²⁹Is God only the God of the Jews? Is he not also the God of those who are not Jews? ³⁰Of course he is, because there is only one God. He will make Jews right with him by their faith, and he will also make those who are not Jews right with him through their faith. ³¹So do we destroy the law by following the way of faith? No! Faith causes us to be what the law truly wants.

¹So what can we say that Abraham, the father of our people, learned about faith? ²If Abraham was made right by the things he did, he had a reason to brag. But this is not God's view, ³because the Scripture says, "Abraham believed God, and God accepted Abraham's faith, and that faith made him right with God."
⁴When people work, their pay is not given as a gift, but as something earned. ⁵But people cannot do any work that will make them right with God. So they must trust in him, who makes even evil people right in his sight. Then God accepts their faith, and that makes them right with him.

Romans 3:27—4:5

7. How would you describe "faith" to a child?

_____

_____

_____

_____

_____

8. What kinds of things do you think hinder our faith?

_____

_____

_____

_____

9. How widespread do you think legalism is in our culture today?

_____

_____

_____

_____

My Reflections

If you have never known the crush of legalism, be grateful. You have been spared.

Others of you haven't. Legalism is slow torture, suffocation of the spirit, amputation of one's dreams. Legalism is just enough religion to keep you, but not enough to nourish you. Your diet is rules and standards. No vitamins. No taste. No zest. Just bland, predictable religion.

—Max

Journal

In what areas of my life has my spirituality been dry or predictable? What changes can I make?

_____

_____

_____

_____

_____

_____

_____

_____

_____

_____

_____

_____

_____

_____

_____

_____

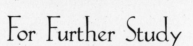

For Further Study

To study more about the law and grace, read Luke 5:33–39; John 1:17; John 7:21–24; Romans 4:16; Romans 5:20; Romans 6:14–15; Galatians 2:21; Galatians 3:18; Galatians 5:4.

Additional Questions

10. What evidence do you see around you that people are prone to rule-making?

_____

_____

_____

_____

_____

_____

11. How would you describe the relationship between the law and grace?

_____

_____

_____

_____

_____

_____

12. Why are we prone to think that we can get God's approval through good works?

_____

_____

_____

_____

_____

_____

Additional Thoughts

_____

69

_____

_____

_____

_____

_____

_____

_____

_____

_____

_____

_____

_____

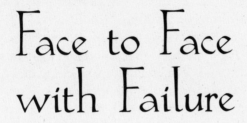

Face to Face with Failure

The most difficult journey is back to the place where you failed.

Jesus knows that. That's why he volunteers to go along. "The first outing was solo; this time I'll be with you. Try it again, this time with me on board." —Max Lucado

71

1. If failure were a color, what color do you think it would it be? Why?

_____

_____

_____

_____

_____

_____

_____

_____

A Moment with Max

Max shares these insights with us in his book *He Still Moves Stones*.

Peter is in the boat, on the lake. Once again he's fished all night. Once again the sea has surrendered nothing.

His thoughts are interrupted by a shout from the shore. "Catch any fish?" Peter and John look up. Probably a villager. "No!" they yell. "Try the other side!" So out sails the net. Peter wraps the rope around his wrist to wait.

But there is no wait. The rope pulls taut and the net catches. Peter begins to bring in the net; reaching down, pulling up, reaching down, pulling up. He's so intense with the task, he misses the message.

John doesn't. "It's the Lord, Peter. It's the Lord!"

Peter plunges into the water, swims to the shore, and stumbles out wet and shivering and stands in front of the friend he betrayed. Jesus has prepared a bed of coals. Both are aware of the last time Peter had stood near a fire. Peter had failed God, but God had come to him.

For one of the few times in his life, Peter is silent. What words would suffice? The moment is too holy for words. God is offering breakfast to the friend who betrayed him. And Peter is once again finding grace at Galilee.

72

2. How do you imagine Peter felt when he saw Jesus for the first time after denying him?

_____

_____

_____

_____

3. Describe a time when you, like Peter, were too preoccupied or busy to recognize God's presence with you.

_____

_____

_____

_____

A Message from the Word

¹Later, Jesus showed himself to his followers again—this time at Lake Galilee. This is how he showed himself: ²Some of the followers were together: Simon Peter, Thomas (called Didymus), Nathanael from Cana in Galilee, the two sons of Zebedee, and two other followers. ³Simon Peter said, "I am going out to fish."

The others said, "We will go with you." So they went out and got into the boat. They fished that night but caught nothing.

⁴Early the next morning Jesus stood on the shore, but the followers did not know it was Jesus. ⁵Then he said to them, "Friends, did you catch any fish?"

They answered, "No."

⁶He said, "Throw your net on the right side of the boat, and you will find some." So they did, and they caught so many fish they could not pull the net back into the boat.

⁷The follower whom Jesus loved said to Peter, "It is the Lord!" When Peter heard him say this, he wrapped his coat around himself. (Peter had taken his clothes off.) Then he jumped into the water. ⁸The other followers went to shore in the boat, dragging the net full of fish. They were not very far from shore, only about a hundred yards. ⁹When the followers stepped out of the boat and onto the shore, they saw a fire of hot coals. There were fish on the fire, and there was bread.

¹⁰Then Jesus said, "Bring some of the fish you just caught."

¹¹Simon Peter went into the boat and pulled the net to the shore. It was full of big fish, one hundred fifty-three in all, but even though there were so many, the net did not tear.

John 2:1-11

73

4. What lesson do you think Jesus wanted Peter to learn from this experience?

_____

_____

_____

_____

5. Why do you think Peter was in a hurry to see Jesus after his failure?

_____

_____

6. What keeps us from running to Jesus after we have failed?

More from the Word

[54]They arrested Jesus, and led him away, and brought him into the house of the high priest. Peter followed far behind them. [55]After the soldiers started a fire in the middle of the courtyard and sat together, Peter sat with them. [56]A servant girl saw Peter sitting there in the firelight, and looking closely at him, she said, "This man was also with him."

[57]But Peter said this was not true; he said, "Woman, I don't know him."

[58]A short time later, another person saw Peter and said, "You are also one of them."

But Peter said, "Man, I am not!"

[59]About an hour later, another man insisted, "Certainly this man was with him, because he is from Galilee, too."

[60]But Peter said, "Man, I don't know what you are talking about!"

At once, while Peter was still speaking, a rooster crowed. [61]Then the Lord turned and looked straight at Peter. And Peter remembered what the Lord had said: "Before the rooster crows this day, you will say three times that you don't know me."

Luke 22:54-61

7. What personal fears do you think caused Peter to deny Jesus?

_____

_____

8. What kinds of fears motivate us to compromise our convictions?

_____

_____

_____

_____

9. How do you imagine this experience impacted Peter for the rest of his life?

_____

_____

75

_____

_____

_____

My Reflections

It's just you and God. You and God both know what you did. And neither one of you is proud of it. What do you do?

You might consider doing what Peter did. Stand in God's presence. Stand in his sight. Stand still and wait. Sometimes that's all a soul can do. Too repentant to speak, but too hopeful to leave—we just stand.

Stand amazed.

He has come back.

He invites you to try again. This time, with him.

—Max

Journal

What failure in my life do I need to revisit with a greater awareness of God's presence?

For Further Study

To study more about failure, read Genesis 3:1-24; 1 Samuel 4:1-22; Psalm 51:1-17; Proverbs 15:22; Romans 15:1.

Additional Questions

10. Describe someone you know who has learned from failure.

_____

_____

_____

_____

_____

_____

_____

11. What keeps us from admitting our failures to God and those we have wronged?

_____

_____

_____

_____

_____

12. Why do you think there is such a stigma on admitting failure when we know that even the most successful people fail along the way?

_____

_____

_____

_____

_____

_____

Additional Thoughts

_____

_____

_____

_____

_____

_____

_____

_____

_____

_____

_____

Does God Sweat the Small Stuff?

What matters to you, matters to God.

You probably think that's true when it comes to the big stuff. When it comes to the major-league difficulties like death, disease, sin, and disaster—you know that God cares.

But what about the smaller things? What about grouchy bosses or flat tires or lost dogs? What about broken dishes, late flights, tooth-aches, or a crashed hard disk? Do these matter to God?   *—Max Lucado*

1. What is one seemingly insignificant thing that can wreck your entire day?

_____

_____

_____

_____

_____

_____

A Moment with Max

Max shares these insights with us in his book *He Still Moves Stones*.

He's got a universe to run. He's got the planets to keep balanced and presidents and kings to watch over. He's got wars to worry with and famines to fix. Who am I to tell him about my ingrown toenail?

I'm glad you asked. Let me tell you who you are. In fact, let me proclaim who you are.

You are an heir of God.

You are eternal.

You have a crown.

You are a holy priest.

You were chosen before the creation.

But more than any of the above—more significant than any title or position—is the simple fact that you are God's child. "The Father has loved us so much that we are called children of God. And we really are his children" (1 John 3:1).

I love that last phrase! "We really are his children." It's as if John knew some of us would shake our heads and say, "Naw, not me. Mother Teresa, maybe. Billy Graham, all right. But not me." If those are your feelings, John added that phrase for you.

"We really are his children."

As a result, if something is important to you, it's important to God.

2. Explain what it means to you to know that you were chosen by God before creation.

_____

_____

_____

_____

_____

3. Why is it so difficult to believe that God cares about the small details of our lives?

_____

_____

A Message from the Word

[1]Two days later there was a wedding in the town of Cana in Galilee. Jesus' mother was there, [2]and Jesus and his followers were also invited to the wedding. [3]When all the wine was gone, Jesus' mother said to him, "They have no more wine."

[4]Jesus answered, "Dear woman, why come to me? My time has not yet come."

[5]His mother said to the servants, "Do whatever he tells you to do."

[6]In that place there were six stone water jars that the Jews used in their washing ceremony. Each jar held about twenty or thirty gallons.

[7]Jesus said to the servants, "Fill the jars with water." So they filled the jars to the top.

[8]Then he said to them, "Now take some out and give it to the master of the feast."

So they took the water to the master. [9]When he tasted it, the water had become wine. He did not know where the wine came from, but the servants who had brought the water knew. The master of the wedding called the bridegroom [10]and said to him, "People always serve the best wine first. Later, after the guests have been drinking awhile, they serve the cheaper wine. But you have saved the best wine till now."

[11]So in Cana of Galilee Jesus did his first miracle. There he showed his glory, and his followers believed in him.

John 2:1-11

4. Why do you think Jesus' mother wanted to involve him in the problem faced by the wedding hosts?

_____

_____

_____

_____

5. What impact did this miracle have on Jesus' disciples?

_____

_____

_____

_____

6. Why do you think Jesus chose to reveal his power and glory at this time and place?

_____

_____

_____

_____

More from the Word

[25]"So I tell you, don't worry about the food or drink you need to live, or about the clothes you need for your body. Life is more than food, and the body is more than clothes. [26]Look at the birds in the air. They don't plant or harvest or store food in barns, but your heavenly Father feeds them. And you know that you are worth much more than the birds. [27]You cannot add any time to your life by worrying about it.

[28]"And why do you worry about clothes? Look at how the lilies in the field grow. They don't work or make clothes for themselves. [29]But I tell you that even Solomon with his riches was not dressed as beautifully as one of these flowers. [30]God clothes the grass in the field, which is alive today but tomorrow is thrown into the fire. So you can be even more sure that God will clothe you. Don't have so little faith! [31]Don't worry and say, 'What will we eat?' or 'What will we drink?' or 'What will we wear?' [32]The people who don't know God keep trying to get these things, and your Father in heaven knows you need them."

Matthew 6:25-32

7. Which of life's basic needs do you think people worry about the most?

_____

_____

_____

_____

8. If God knows our needs, why do we worry about them?

_____

_____

_____

_____

9. How does believing that you matter to God impact your attitude about your basic needs?

_____

_____

_____

_____

My Reflections

So go ahead. Tell God what hurts. Talk to him. He won't turn you away. He won't think it's silly. "For our high priest is able to understand our weaknesses. When he lived on earth, he was tempted in every way that we are, but he did not sin. Let us then, feel very sure that we can come before God's throne where there is grace." (Heb. 4:15–16).

Does God care about the little things in our lives? You better believe it. If it matters to you, it matters to him.

—Max

Journal

If I was a child sitting on God's lap, what would I tell him about the hurts in my life?

_____

_____

_____

_____

_____

_____

_____

_____

_____

_____

_____

_____

_____

_____

_____

For Further Study

To study more about God's concern for you, read Exodus 3:7-10; Joshua 1:5; Psalm 13:6; Psalm 23:1-6; Daniel 6:22; Matthew 11:28-30.

Additional Questions

10. Name two things that you really, really believe might be too small for God to be concerned with.

_____

_____

_____

_____

_____

_____

_____

11. What amazes you the most about God's concern for your life?

_____

_____

_____

_____

_____

_____

12. Why is it hard for us to sometimes show concern for the little things in each other's lives?

_____

_____

_____

_____

_____

_____

Additional Thoughts

_____

_____

_____

_____

_____

_____

_____

_____

_____

_____

_____

Seeing What Heaven Sees

An example of faith was found on the wall of a concentration camp. On it a prisoner had carved the words:

> *I believe in the sun, even though it doesn't shine,*
> *I believe in love, even when it isn't shown,*
> *I believe in God, even when he doesn't speak.*

I try to imagine the person who etched those words. What hand could have cut such a conviction? What eyes could have seen good in such horror?

There is only one answer. Eyes that chose to see the unseen. —Max Lucado

1. Who has inspired you to believe in the unseen?

_____

_____

_____

A Moment with Max

Max shares these insights with us in his book *He Still Moves Stones*.

The Jairus we see in this story is not the clear-sighted, black-frocked, nicely groomed civic leader. He is instead a blind man begging for a gift. He fell at Jesus' feet, "saying again and again, 'My daughter is dying. Please come and put your hands on her so she will be healed and will live.'" (Mark 5:23).

He doesn't barter with Jesus. He doesn't negotiate. He doesn't make excuses. He just pleads.

There are times in life when everything you have to offer is nothing compared to what you are asking to receive. Jairus is at such a point. What could a man offer in exchange for his child's life? So there are no games. No haggling. No masquerades. The situation is starkly simple: Jairus is blind to the future and Jesus knows the future. So Jairus asks for his help.

And Jesus, who loves the honest heart, goes to give it.

Jesus compels Jairus to see the unseen. When Jesus says, "Just believe . . . ," He is imploring, "Don't limit your possibilities to the visible. Don't listen only for the audible. Don't be controlled by the logical. Believe there is more to life than meets the eye!"

92

2. Think of a time when you wanted something so much that you were willing to beg for it. Describe your feelings at that time.

_____

_____

_____

_____

3. What are the complexities of "believing there is more to life than meets the eye"?

_____

_____

_____

_____

A Message from the Word

When Jesus went in the boat back to the other side of the lake, a large crowd gathered around him there. [22]A leader of the synagogue, named Jairus, came there, saw Jesus, and fell at his feet. [23]He begged Jesus, saying again and again, "My daughter is dying. Please come and put your hands on her so she will be healed and will live." [24]So Jesus went with him.

A large crowd followed Jesus and pushed very close around him.

While Jesus was still speaking, some people came from the house of the synagogue leader. They said, "Your daughter is dead. There is no need to bother the teacher anymore."

[36]But Jesus paid no attention to what they said. He told the synagogue leader, "Don't be afraid; just believe."

[37]Jesus let only Peter, James, and John the brother of James go with him. [38]When they came to the house of the synagogue leader, Jesus found many people there making lots of noise and crying loudly. [39]Jesus entered the house and said to them, "Why are you crying and making so much noise? The child is not dead, only asleep." [40]But they laughed at him. So, after throwing them out of the house, Jesus took the child's father and mother and his three followers into the room where the child was. [41]Taking hold of the girl's hand, he said to her, "*Talitha, koum!*" (This means, "Young girl, I tell you to stand up!") [42]At once the girl stood right up and began walking. (She was twelve years old.) Everyone was completely amazed. [43]Jesus gave them strict orders not to tell people about this. Then he told them to give the girl something to eat.

Mark 5:21-24; 35-43

93

4. What lesson can you learn from Jairus' example?

_____

_____

_____

_____

5. When do the words "Don't be afraid, just believe" seem like not enough?

_____

_____

_____

_____

_____

6. What would you say is the single most difficult thing about putting your
faith in God?

_____

_____

_____

_____

More from the Word

[16]So we do not give up. Our physical body is becoming older and weaker,
but our spirit inside us is made new every day. [17]We have small troubles for
a while now, but they are helping us gain an eternal glory that is much
greater than the troubles. [18]We set our eyes not on what we see but on
what we cannot see. What we see will last only a short time, but what we
cannot see will last forever.

[1]We know that our body—the tent we live in here on earth—will be
destroyed. But when that happens, God will have a house for us. It will not
be a house made by human hands; instead, it will be a home in heaven that
will last forever. [2]But now we groan in this tent. We want God to give us our
heavenly home, [3]because it will clothe us so we will not be naked. [4]While
we live in this body, we have burdens, and we groan. We do not want to be
naked, but we want to be clothed with our heavenly home. Then this body
that dies will be fully covered with life. [5]This is what God made us for, and
he has given us the Spirit to be a guarantee for this new life.

[6]So we always have courage. We know that while we live in this body, we are
away from the Lord. [7]We live by what we believe, not by what we can see.

2 Corinthians 4:16—5:7

7. How is your life different when you live by faith rather than sight?

_____

_____

_____

_____

8. What evidence have you seen that there is a part of us that longs for heaven?

_____

_____

_____

9. In what ways does a heavenly perspective change the way we look at our earthly circumstances?

_____

_____

_____

_____

My Reflections

Jesus is asking Jairus to see the unseen. To make a choice. Either to live by the facts or to see by faith. When tragedy strikes we, too, are left to choose what we see. We can see either the hurt or the Healer.

The choice is ours.

Mark it down—God knows living by faith and not by sight doesn't come naturally. And I think that's one reason he raised Jairus's daughter from the dead. Not for her sake—she was better off in heaven. But for our sake—to teach us that heaven sees when we trust.

—Max

Journal

How can I turn my eyes from the hurt in my life to the Healer?

For Further Study

To study more about faith, read Matthew 8:8-10; Matthew 9:20-22; Luke 17:5-6; Romans 1:17; Romans 4:4-6; 2 Cor. 5:7; Galatians 2:16; Galatians 3:14.

Additional Questions

10. What are the unseen things that encourage your faith the most?

_____

_____

_____

_____

_____

_____

_____

11. How can believers help one another to live by faith?

_____

_____

_____

_____

_____

_____

12. What practical steps can you take to strengthen your faith?

_____

_____

_____

_____

_____

Additional Thoughts

_____

_____

_____

_____

_____

_____

_____

_____

_____

_____

_____

_____

_____

Why God Does What He Does

Each of us knows what it's like to search the night for light. Not outside a stable, but perhaps outside an emergency room. On the gravel of a roadside. On the manicured grass of a cemetery. We've asked our questions. We've questioned God's plan. And we've wondered why God does what he does. —Max Lucado

101

1. What Bible character had to ignore what seemed to be common sense to obey God?

_____

_____

_____

_____

_____

_____

_____

A Moment with Max

Max shares these insights with us in his book *He Still Moves Stones*.

The Bible is a fence full of knotholes through which we can peek but not see the whole picture. It's a scrapbook of snapshots capturing people in encounters with God, but not always recording the result.

You'll find them in every chapter about every person. But nothing stirs so many questions as does the birth of Christ. Characters appear and disappear before we can ask them anything. The innkeeper too busy to welcome God—did he ever learn who he turned away? The shepherds—did they ever hum the song the angels sang? The wise men who followed the star— what was it like to worship a toddler? And Joseph, especially Joseph. I've got questions for Joseph.

Did you and Jesus arm wrestle? Did he ever let you win?

Did you ever look up from your prayers and see Jesus listening?

What ever happened to the wise men?

What ever happened to you?

We don't know what happened to Joseph. His role in Act 1 is so crucial that we expect to see him the rest of the drama—but with the exception of a short scene with twelve-year-old Jesus in Jerusalem, he never reappears. The rest of his life is left to speculation, and we are left with our questions.

2. What questions would you want to ask Joseph?

_____

_____

_____

_____

_____

3. Describe some of the challenges you imagine Joseph faced in raising Jesus, the Son of God.

_____

_____

_____

_____

A Message from the Word

¹⁸This is how the birth of Jesus Christ came about. His mother Mary was engaged to marry Joseph, but before they married, she learned she was pregnant by the power of the Holy Spirit. ¹⁹Because Mary's husband, Joseph, was a good man, he did not want to disgrace her in public, so he planned to divorce her secretly.

²⁰While Joseph thought about these things, an angel of the Lord came to him in a dream. The angel said, "Joseph, descendant of David, don't be afraid to take Mary as your wife, because the baby in her is from the Holy Spirit. ²¹She will give birth to a son, and you will name him Jesus, because he will save his people from their sins."

²²All this happened to bring about what the Lord had said through the prophet: ²³"The virgin will be pregnant. She will have a son, and they will name him Immanuel," which means "God is with us."

²⁴When Joseph woke up, he did what the Lord's angel had told him to do. Joseph took Mary as his wife, ²⁵but he did not have sexual relations with her until she gave birth to the son. And Joseph named him Jesus."

Matthew 1:18–25

4. What do you think gave Joseph the courage to go through with his marriage to Mary?

_____

_____

_____

_____

_____

5. What are some other ways Joseph could have responded to this situation besides obedience?

_____

_____

_____

6. What things did Joseph have to sacrifice to take part in God's plan? What did he gain?

More from the Word

[35]Women received their dead relatives raised back to life. Others were tortured and refused to accept their freedom so they could be raised from the dead to a better life. [36]Some were laughed at and beaten. Others were put in chains and thrown into prison. [37]They were stoned to death, they were cut in half, and they were killed with swords. Some wore the skins of sheep and goats. They were poor, abused, and treated badly. [38]The world was not good enough for them! They wandered in deserts and mountains, living in caves and holes in the earth.

[39]All these people are known for their faith, but none of them received what God had promised. [40]God planned to give us something better so that they would be made perfect, but only together with us.

[1]We have around us many people whose lives tell us what faith means. So let us run the race that is before us and never give up. We should remove from our lives anything that would get in the way and the sin that so easily holds us back. [2]Let us look only to Jesus, the One who began our faith and who makes it perfect. He suffered death on the cross. But he accepted the shame as if it were nothing because of the joy that God put before him. And now he is sitting at the right side of God's throne. [3]Think about Jesus' example. He held on while wicked people were doing evil things to him. So do not get tired and stop trying.

Hebrews 11:35—12:3

7. How would you describe the faith of the martyrs listed in this passage?

_____

_____

_____

8. What impact does the testimony of these people have on you?

_____

_____

_____

_____

9. What things interfere with our ability to finish the race well?

_____

_____

_____

_____

My Reflections

What about you? Just like Joseph, you can't see the whole picture. Just like Joseph your task is to see that Jesus is brought into your part of your world. And just like Joseph you have a choice: to obey or disobey. Because Joseph obeyed, God used him to change the world.

Can he do the same with you?

God still looks for Josephs today. Men and women who believe that God is not through with this world. Common people who serve an uncommon God.

Will you be that kind of person? Will you serve . . . even when you don't understand?

—Max

Journal

What step of faith is God asking me to take today?

For Further Study

To study more about submitting to God's plan, read Psalm 2:11-12; Proverbs 21:21; Matthew 6:24; Matthew 20:25-28; Galatians 5:13; Ephes. 6:5-8.

Additional Questions

10. Why would God ask us to do something we don't understand?

_____

_____

_____

_____

_____

11. How do you know when to trust God even when it doesn't make sense?

_____

_____

_____

_____

_____

_____

12. How can Scripture and the advice of other believers help us determine God's leading in our lives?

_____

_____

_____

_____

_____

_____

Additional Thoughts

_____

_____

_____

_____

_____

_____

_____

_____

_____

_____

_____

_____

110

When is Good, Good Enough?

Most of us think we are "basically good." Decent, hardworking folk. Most of us have a list to prove it.

"I pay my bills."

"I love my spouse and kids."

"I attend church."

"I'm better than Hitler."

"I'm basically good."

Most of us have a list. There is a purpose for the list: To prove we are good. But there is a problem with the list: None of us is good enough. —Max Lucado

1. What comments or phrases do people use to justify their own worth and goodness?

_____

_____

_____

_____

A Moment with Max

Max shares these insights with us in his book *He Still Moves Stones*.

So much for lists. So much for being "basically good."

Then how do you go to heaven? If no one is good, if no list is sufficient, if no achievements are adequate, how can a person be saved?

No question is more crucial. To hear Jesus answer it, let's ponder the last encounter between Jesus and two criminals. All three are being crucified.

One of the criminals who hung there hurled insults at him: "Aren't you the Christ? Then save yourself and us" (Luke 23:39).

The heart of this thief remains hard. The presence of Christ crucified means nothing to him. He expects his chorus to be harmonized from the other cross. It isn't. Instead, it is challenged.

"We are punished justly, for we are getting what our deeds deserve. But this man has done nothing wrong" (vv. 40-41).

The core of the gospel in one sentence. The essence of eternity through the mouth of a crook:

I am wrong; Jesus is right.

I have failed; Jesus has not.

I deserve to die; Jesus deserves to live.

2. In your own words, how would you contrast man's righteousness with Christ's?

_____

_____

_____

_____

3. What part does realizing our own inadequacy play in our salvation?

_____

_____

_____

_____

A Message from the Word

³²There were also two criminals led out with Jesus to be put to death. ³³When they came to a place called the Skull, the soldiers crucified Jesus and the criminals—one on his right and the other on his left. ³⁴Jesus said, "Father, forgive them, because they don't know what they are doing."

The soldiers threw lots to decide who would get his clothes. ³⁵The people stood there watching. And the leaders made fun of Jesus, saying, "He saved others. Let him save himself if he is God's Chosen One, the Christ."

³⁶The soldiers also made fun of him, coming to Jesus and offering him some vinegar. ³⁷They said, "If you are the king of the Jews, save yourself!" ³⁸At the top of the cross these words were written: THIS IS THE KING OF THE JEWS.

³⁹One of the criminals on a cross began to shout insults at Jesus: "Aren't you the Christ? Then save yourself and us."

⁴⁰But the other criminal stopped him and said, "You should fear God! You are getting the same punishment he is. ⁴¹We are punished justly, getting what we deserve for what we did. But this man has done nothing wrong." ⁴²Then he said, "Jesus, remember me when you come into your kingdom."

⁴³Jesus said to him, "I tell you the truth, today you will be with me in paradise."

Luke 23:32-43

113

4. If you knew your death was imminent and Christ was at your side, what would you ask of him?

_____

_____

_____

_____

_____

5. How would you summarize the difference between the attitudes of the two thieves?

_____

_____

6. What kinds of inadequacies do we need to face to understand our salvation?

More from the Word

114 ¹Since we have been made right with God by our faith, we have peace with God. This happened through our Lord Jesus Christ, ²who has brought us into that blessing of God's grace that we now enjoy. And we are happy because of the hope we have of sharing God's glory. ³We also have joy with our troubles, because we know that these troubles produce patience. ⁴And patience produces character, and character produces hope. ⁵And this hope will never disappoint us, because God has poured out his love to fill our hearts. He gave us his love through the Holy Spirit, whom God has given to us.

⁶When we were unable to help ourselves, at the moment of our need, Christ died for us, although we were living against God. ⁷Very few people will die to save the life of someone else. Although perhaps for a good person someone might possibly die. ⁸But God shows his great love for us in this way: Christ died for us while we were still sinners.

Romans 5:1-8

7. Why is it crucial for us to understand that we have nothing to bring to God to make us worthy in his eyes?

_____

_____

8. What are we uncomfortable with needing somebody or something?

_____

_____

_____

_____

9. How does the knowledge that you have access to God through Jesus Christ affect your daily routine?

_____

_____

_____

_____

My Reflections

You see, that is you and me on the cross. Naked, desolate, hopeless, and estranged. That is us. That is us asking, "In spite of what I've done, in spite of what you see, is there any way you could remember me when we all get home?"

We don't boast. We don't produce our list. Any sacrifice appears silly when placed before God on a cross.

We, like the thief, have one more prayer. And we, like the thief, pray.

And we, like the thief, hear the voice of grace. Today you will be with me in my kingdom.

And we, like the thief, are able to endure the pain knowing he'll soon take us home.

—Max

Journal

In what ways am I like the thief on the cross?

STEEL, STRUCTURE,
AND ARCHITECTURE

Arne Petter Eggen & Bjørn Normann Sandaker

Introduction by Christian Norberg-Schulz

STEEL, STRUCTURE, AND ARCHITECTURE

Whitney Library of Design
an imprint of Watson-Guptill Publications/New York

51227

Senior Editor: Roberto de Alba
Associate Editor: Micaela Porta
Production Manager: Ellen Greene

First published in the United States in 1995 by Whitney Library of Design, an imprint of Watson-Guptill Publications, a division of BPI Communications, Inc., 1515 Broadway, New York, NY 10036.

Library of Congress Cataloging-in-Publication Data

Eggen, Arne Petter.
    [Stal, struktur og arkitektur. English]
    Steel, structure, and architecture / Arne Petter Eggen & Bjørn
Normann Sandaker; introduction by Christian Norberg-Schulz.
        p.   cm.
    Translation of: Stal, struktur og arkitektur.
    Includes bibliographical references and index.
    ISBN 0-8230-5020-3
    1. Building, Iron and steel. 2. Steel, Structural. I. Sandaker,
Bjørn Normann, 1954–   . II. Title.
    TA684.E33   1995
    624.1'821—dc20   95–16755
                                              CIP

Distributed in the United Kingdom by Phaidon Press, Ltd., 140 Kensington Church Street, London W8 48N, England.
Distributed in Europe (except the United Kingdom, South and Central America, the Caribbean, the Far East, the Southeast, and Central Asia) by Rotovision S.A., Route Suisse 9, CH-1295 Mies, Switzerland.

Manufactured in the United States

First printing, 1995

1 2 3 4 5 6 7 8 9 / 02 01 00 99 98 97 96 95

CONTENTS

Foreword

This book has been written to convey a knowledge of steel as an architectural building material and to inspire students, project planners, and builders to utilize the expressive, technological, and functional qualities of steel. We have approached this material from a broad perspective of steel in architecture. In addition to citing significant international examples of steel architecture, we have included steel in other applications: Furniture, sculpture and bridges can very well be the point of departure for a structural or architectonic idea.

Many years of experience in teaching architecture students have also shown us that steel as a building material is extremely well-suited for instruction. Architectural constructions of steel have a lucidity and precision well suited for teaching statics, design, and detailing.

The initiative for writing this book came from The Norwegian Steel Group and its project, Steel in Building. At that time, The Norwegian Steel Group was the name of an organization of Norwegian steel producers, steel suppliers, and steel workshops. During the entire process, Steel in Building has been not only a willing source of funding but also a driving force that has candidly joined and supported what we present as the book's concept. We want especially to thank board chairman Klaus Eicke as well as the directors of the Steel in Building project, originally Dr. Bjorn Aaasen and later Einar Braathu.

Many have contributed to the completion of this book. We owe deep gratitude to Karin Hagen, Britt Bordnes, Aase Hultgren, Berit Jensen, Anders Kirkhus, and Frode Lunde. We would also like to thank our enthusiastic publisher.

Arne Petter Eggen
Bjørn Normann Sandaker

Oslo, June, 1994

9

The Backbone of Freedom
Christian Norberg-Schulz

Modern architecture is the architecture of freedom. And steel is its backbone. "Freedom," what does it mean in this context? The word stands for a new beginning, a new time, when the world was united and architecture became "global."

The new beginning first manifested itself in London in 1851, in Paxton's Crystal Palace. In this enormous building of iron and glass, nations were gathered to show one another their identities and their creativity. The gathering occurred in a space of "undetermined" dimensions, with the horizon as a boundary and the structure as the prevailing rhythm. This was the way the Crystal Palace expressed modern architecture's basic principles: the "free plan" and the "clear structure."

Mies van der Rohe knew this when he much later said: "A clear structure is the backbone in it all and makes the free plan possible." "Clear structure" doesn't here stand for any building method at all, but means, in principle, a regular skeleton that replaces the bearing walls of earlier days. Le Corbusier shared Mies' conception and showed in his five points for a new architecture that a clear system of pilotis not only releases the plan and the facade, but enables the ground to retain its interdependence and makes the sky accessible from a roof terrace and solarium. This is why freedom meant more for the pioneers than a game of "floating" spatial effects; above all, freedom meant that people could get healthy dwellings in airy "green" cities. "Freedom" also meant a liberation from "form lies" of the past, to use van der Velde's words. What it means is that a building's space, form, and structure finally could be in agreement, thanks to the new materials, initially iron (steel) and glass, and later reinforced concrete. This is why Siegfried Giedion (1888–1968), in his book *Space, Time and Architecture*, spoke of a new "moral" in architecture.

Now, unfortunately, development has not fully confirmed these intentions. The green city certainly did not satisfy all human needs and the free plan applied only to certain building tasks or parts thereof. But as a possibility, freedom is still our hope, and the means is still clear structure! This is why it is important to understand what it really means, that is, what building ought to be in our day.

When forged iron and steel began to be used during the last century, it was in relation to two basic spatial types: the comprehensive hall and the repetitive cell structure (that can be developed either horizontally or vertically). The hall appeared first, in connection with exhibition buildings, railway stations, factories, and warehouses. As an especially magnificent example we have the Galerie des Machines by Dutert and Contamin at the world exhibition in Paris in 1889. This hall was made up of an open row of three-hinged steel arches with a free span of 115 meters! After the big city fire in Chicago in 1871, William Le Baron Jenney developed the multi-storied steel frame, which permitted a rapid and forward-looking reconstruction of the burned city. Jenney's successor, Louis Sullivan, understood what this meant architectonically and in 1896 published his famous work, *The Tall Office Building Artistically Considered*. In it, he expounds on expressing a building's function with the help of its structure.

Between the two world wars, the possibilities of steel were somewhat overshadowed by reinforced concrete. But after Mies van der Rohe emigrated from Berlin to Chicago in 1937, the tradition from Sullivan's time was taken up again. Mies developed both the hall and the repetitive skeleton, initially in connection with the planning of the Illinois Institute of Technology, where he headed up the architecture

arnsworth House,
946–50
rchitect: Mies van der
ohe

*Alumni Memorial
Hall, 1945
Corner detail*

department. For him, as mentioned, structure and space were one, so he sought
make the structure of the building visible. In the "cell" buildings, this meant a nee
for a double structure: a primary, bearing skeleton with fireproof cladding and
secondary, outer skeleton that serves to stiffen the structure and to secure th
windows and tight wall sections. The famous corner from the Alumni Memorial Ha
at IIT (1945) shows how the outer skeleton is non-bearing because it stands on th
brick wall, while the primary columns are just barely visible within the concav
corner. In the project for the administration building at IIT (1944), on the othe
hand, the solution was a large common space with large plate girders stretchir
between the two long walls. These are visible as "plastic" profiles in the er

facades, while the long facades are placed outside as smooth, enveloping surfaces. Later, Mies developed the hall construction further by using large outside frames or trusses from which the roof slab is hung (Crown Hall at IIT and the project for the Mannheim Opera, both 1953).

I mention these famous things because the thought of "clear construction" today is being quickly forgotten. Thus, modern architecture has become the victim of a new historicism in which "form lies" once again are hung outside the actual buildings. Modernism after World War II forgot that it was the architecture of freedom, and instead became the expression of a one-sided, economically instrumental mentality. But that doesn't justify abandoning it's basic principles. They are still valid and the new materials are once again waiting to be used with meaning.

What is steel's essence as a building material? This book shows it. However, a few general comments are also in order. Therefore, let me ask: What does steel want to be? The world "steel section" hints at part of the answer. As a building material, steel appears first and foremost as linear units pieced together to form frames, trusses, and space frames. The combination has two tasks: to provide space for functions and to give form to a character. The construction must be planned and dimensioned in agreement with both requirements. The first calls for horizontal and vertical rhythms, while the other demands that certain section types be combined. This is where we can learn from Mies' IIT buildings. Mies' articulation of the primary and the secondary steel elements and integration of the glass and brick surfaces in the building's envelope represent a study in structurally dependent design that is reminiscent of the post and beam and half-timber structures of earlier days. Mies also said that "there is no better example for young architects than the old wooden buildings."

Put more generally, will steel "stand," "span," "branch out," and "be composed?" Thanks to its material properties, it easily "stands" freely; in fact, Giedion has compared the pin-jointed bases of the Galerie des Machines to a ballerina on her tip-toes. Such a dynamic is possible when the structure is rigid, while the fixed pillars of Mies' 1962 National Gallery in Berlin displace the lightness up under them. However, in both cases the relation to the ground and sky is expressed with anthropomorphic character. Span and ramification are just as important, something already shown in Horta's art nouveau skeletons and in Chedanne's "Le Parisien" (1904). Composition means, among other things, the aforementioned combination of steel sections that replace the prehistoric use of stylistic elements with structural joints. All styles that had a structural origin were limited by the material's ability to withstand stress. With steel all the innate structural possibilities are realizable.

National Gallery, Berlin, 1962 Architect: Mies van der Rohe

Let me finally emphasize that architecture is the art of building. Architecture is not adornment, but rather a concrete realization of rhythm and tension. Modern architecture gave special emphasis to structural honesty. But it is clear that "honesty" is not an exclusive property of steel and concrete. Mies said that "architecture begins when you place two bricks carefully one on top of the other." The new materials made it possible to "destroy the box," to use a Frank Lloyd Wright expression. Recent developments have confirmed the importance of this, but have also shown that "the box" is still necessary in many contexts. The "architecture of freedom" does not imply chaos, but a freedom of choice: the choice between "box" and "free plan." This choice presupposes a "backbone" that ensures the unity of structure, space, and form.

IRON, ARCHITECTURE, AND HISTORY

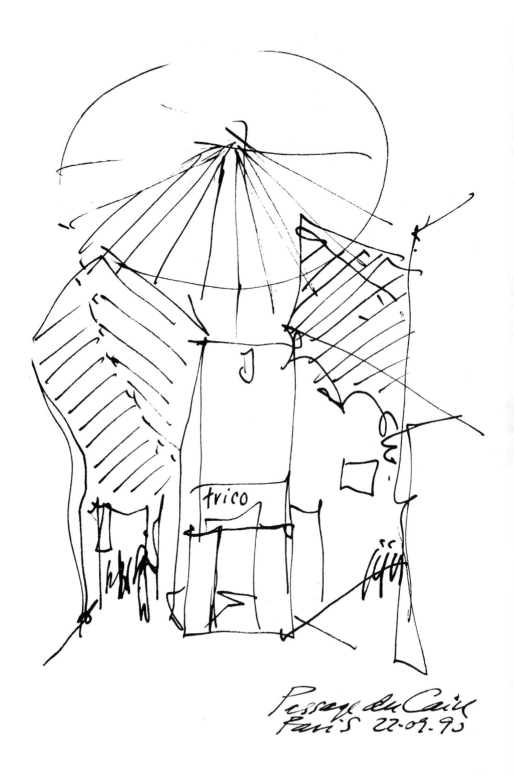

Passage du Caire,
Paris, 1799

The history of iron's entry into architecture is an exciting one. It stretches roughly over the past 200 years, and seen in perspective it is the story of a conscious wish that gradually became a necessity. Iron has gone from a material of secondary importance to become one of our most useful structural materials. Beginning as substitutes for stone and logs, iron and steel have little by little found their own structural and architectonic expression. This expression, however, has not reached—nor will it reach—a final form, for iron's architectonic potential is practically inexhaustible.

This introduction does not give a complete overview of the architectural history of iron and steel, nor does it include the most important buildings, those that had the greatest influence at their time or subsequently. Rather, it is a brief look at a fascinating development, a short story about individual people who, with the approval (or, more often, disapproval) of society, were able to construct buildings that today serve as reference points for designing and building in our own time. These buildings tell of a continuous search for innovations in iron and steel, for an architecture based on the material's own values, worked into a functional and local contextual reality. To understand the use of steel in our day it is useful to be acquainted with the building tradition of the Iron Age.

An early example of the use of iron in architecture can be found in the east facade of the Louvre museum in Paris. The architect Claude Perrault (1613–1688) erected this wing in the 1670s and used wrought iron rods as reinforcement in a masonry entablature. Engineer Jean Rondolet (1734–1823) did the same thing when about 100 years later, he designed the structure for architect Germain Soufflot's (1713–1780) Ste. Genevieve Church, later called the Pantheon, in Paris. This opened the way for utilizing iron and changing the dimensions of classical architecture. At the time iron was not being used as an exposed structural element, but nonetheless paved the way to the realization of an altered architectural expression.

New materials first appeared, as one can expect, in building types that did not have long traditions of their own. This is why we first find iron in the new factory structures in Great Britain and on the Continent, in cotton mills, textile mills warehouses, and packing houses. Iron found an urban foothold in the many glass-covered galleries that were erected in Europe from about 1800 to 1850. In a similar way, the new structures by engineers—primarily bridges—also served as stepping stones. The outstanding monuments, Ironbridge (1779) and Pont des Arts (1803), are discussed in a separate chapter on bridges.

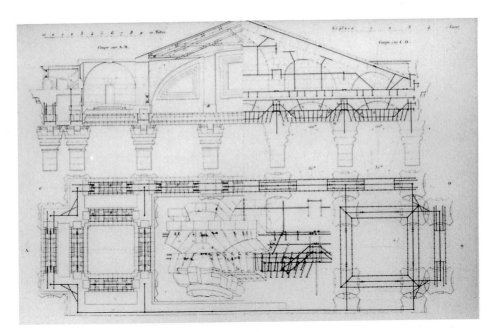

We will begin here with a building that has remained standing as one of the very first in which an architect and an engineer collaborated creatively in the development of the project: Halle au Blé, built as a grain silo for Paris but now known as the Bourse de Commerce, was given an iron cupola in 1811 that covered an inner courtyard and significantly augmented the hall's storage capacity. However, the building began a good deal earlier. The circular stone building was raised during the 1760s and was supplemented by a wooden cupola over the courtyard 20 years later. The cupola was the biggest and lightest in the world at that time, but burned down in 1802. It was decided that a new cupola should be installed, but that it was to be fireproof. The suggestion to build a cupola construction in the form of a brick shell had to be abandoned because the existing building wouldn't stand the load. Therefore, architect François Belanger (1744–1818) suggested using iron. The form was determined by the burned wooden construction, with adjustments recommended by the designer of the Pantheon, Jean Rondolet. Engineer F. Brunet was contacted by the architect to collaborate on the task. Brunet writes: "M. Belanger...has engaged me to undertake the necessary calculations for making the wood models that will guide completion of the iron casting."[1] The calculations Brunet referred to were not static ones. This theoretical foundation was still not in place. The task concerned the precise design of the individual cast iron arches which made up the cupola—51 in all—and was thus a geometric problem. Each arch was cast in four parts and bolted together. Therefore, it was difficult to consider adapting elements during the building process, and absolute precision was needed.

17

With a span of almost 40 meters, the Halle au Blé and its iron cupola was a formidable achievement. We notice that the individual arches are formed with two curved elements at a distance from one another, but with cross connections at regular intervals. This ensures a rigid structure without excessive use of materials, and represents a recognition of a work process based on experience and knowledge that preceeded Navier's theoretical formulation of the bending problem. Elias Cornell sums up Halle au Blé this way: "The engineer had reached a precision that competed with the finest machinery. The architect had reached the goal for the clarity that Soufflot had begun to seek with his Pantheon. Together they had realized the building as a true synthesis, the absolute architecture and building technology, that their colleagues had dreamed of for a generation.[2]

With the growth of the railroad in the 1800s, a new building type made its appearance: the railroad station. This was a building type that of necessity made structural innovations, testing new solutions and new uses of material. Especially in connection with railway lines' end stations it became necessary to build large train halls providing the most comfortable entraining and detraining possible and protected from precipitation. The hall structures are thus characterized by large, freely spanning roof surfaces over the railroad tracks with fixed rows of supporting pillars along the platforms.

The railway stations are also exponents for the unclear conditions that architects of the 1800s had to work under: The facades of station buildings might be built as variations of eclectic historicism with little visual or material relationship to the train hall, which was that part of the station building in which the new structural possibilities of the day were tested. To put it simply, we can say that the architect and engineer shared the building project between them, with the architect taking charge of the representative, outward functions and the relationship to the city's space and facades, while the engineer was needed for his knowledge to help solve the problems associated with the great spans. The train halls offered new structural, functional and formal problems that could not be understood by looking back historically.

The Gare St. Lazare in Paris, from 1851-52, is a typical example. The building was erected by engineer Eugene Flachat (1802–1873) and architect Alfred Arman (1805–1888). The interior of the train hall was immortalized by Claude Monet in number of oil paintings. Above the tracks are stretched series of so-called Poloncea trusses, column constructions based on inverted roof trusses of wrought iron and cast iron of a very light and elegant character. The structure's tension rods are made of wrought iron, while the bearing elements are of cast iron, and all components are formed so that material use and manufacturing process are easily distinguishable. Large glass sections in the roof surface furnish the hall with daylight and the structure's minimal dimensions allow as much light as possible to reach the tracks. The train hall in Gare St. Lazare is a very large space with qualities that were appreciated in its day both among the public and by Napoleon III.[3]

With the works of architect Henri Labrouste (1801–1875) iron as a building material was introduced in earnest in representative public buildings. Of the Biblioteque Saint-Genevieve (1843–1850), Siegfried Giedion has this to say: Here Labrouste "made the first attempt at utilizing a construction of cast iron and wrought iron from the foundation through to the roof in the construction of a public building."[4] The library was built on a long narrow lot and has a ground plan of about 21 x 85 m / 70 x 283'. Labrouste's choice of iron as structural material was based on a desire to best utilize the area by making the bearing structures as slim as possible, and to reduce the risk in case of fire.

The large reading room was covered by two lengthwise barrel vaults, vaults formed by repeating arches. Wrought iron arches span between the outer walls and the mid axis, which is borne by a row of 18 thin cast-iron columns. The arches are noteworthy constructions that represent a fusion of statics and ornamentation that are both charming and justifiable. Acanthus vines coil themselves between the upper and lower booms and form diagonals in a truss pattern. In this way the need for structural strength and a moderate decor are met in one and the same element.

This represents a transitional phenomenon toward more cultivated forms of construction, and was entirely in keeping with Labrouste's ideals, namely that ornamentation had to be derived from the structure itself and be meaningful but expressive.

At the same time Labrouste erected the Ste. Genevieve library, the French architect and architectural theoretician, Leonce Reynaud (1803–1880), wrote: "The new material offered us [iron] necessitates new forms and new proportions, because it is

basically different from all the [materials] that have so far been provided to us to work with. What applies to stone will in no way apply to iron."[5]

The Biblioteque National (1858–1868) is considered Labrouste's major work, the one in which he reaches his full development. To an ever increasing extent, the enormous growth of book publication in the 1800s called for libraries that had to separate their reading rooms from their book-storage space. The plan for the reading room itself is basically a square with one of its sides rounded off by a circle segment. The space is covered by nine light cupola constructions that rest on iron arches stretched between sixteen cast-iron pillars. Compared to Ste. Genevieve, the arches are formed with a more refined truss principle, with straight cross pillars between the booms and with a cross. Iron rivets holding the sections together lend the structural material a rich texture, and appear as a decoration provided by the "structure itself." The actual cupola has round openings in the crown, and the surfaces are covered with glazed tiles that reflect natural light.

*Facing page: Le
Parisien Liberé, Paris,
1904
Architect: G. Chedanne*

*Right: Chocolaterie
Menier
Iron skeleton
supplemented with
multicolored brick*

24

There is little doubt that Labrouste saw his two library buildings as an architectural homage to the book. With them he gave a powerful reply to Victor Hugo, who 20 years earlier, in 1831, had written that architecture was "dead for all time, killed by the printed book, killed because it is less constant, killed because it is much more costly."[6]

As far as we know, the oldest fully complete building in the world with an iron skeleton is a large, imposing factory building that is still in use: the Menier Chocolate Factory in Noisiel-sur-Marne, outside Paris. In this building—which from a material point of view is a beautiful union of iron and brick—iron alone, for the first time, bears both the vertical and horizontal loads. The multi-colored brick is merely complimentary. The Menier Chocolate Factory (1871–1872) is designed by the architect Jules Saulnier (1817–1881). Placed right in the middle of the Marne River, it utilizes the current to power its turbines. The building rests on four hollow iron girders running lengthwise that span the foundations in the river. The skeleton itself consist of columns, horizontal beams, and diagonal buttresses. The columns are joined in cross-section by steel beams via powerful, rounded frame corners that provide the cross buttressing. The iron sections consist of two joined T-sections that form H-sections and envelope the bricks. The method of construction clearly shows features borrowed from the French tradition of wooden framework.

Contemporary buildings that were meant to have a formal or representative character often were given richly ornamented facades. In this building, the facades are all flat. Saulnier explains this by referring to the structural system: The construction, quite naturally, provides a surface that is completely flat from roof to foundation, without either horizontal or vertical projections. We can interpret this as a precursor to the ornament-free, flat facades of modern architecture, and it is interesting that the will to carry through the expressive simplification this implies is present simultaneously with new construction possibilities. The only concession Saulnier has made consists of an extensive use of multi-colored, glazed bricks and the beautiful medallions depicting the cocoa plant, which symbolizes the activity the building houses.

The office building in rue Saint-Marc, No. 25, in Paris stands as a characteristic representative of the entry of iron and steel and their expansion in the urban environment. It dates from 1894 and is designed by architect Louis Thalheimer (1859–1910). Common to this type of building is the combination of steel columns, steel beams, and weight-bearing brick walls in the facades. Facing the street, the building has a facade of natural stone, while facing the back courtyard the facade is of second-hand brick. At the same time, steel gradually became a bigger part of facades, something that made possible greater glass surfaces and more access for light.

Facing page: Le Parisien Liberé, Paris, 1904
Architect: G. Chedanne

The steel columns in rue Saint-Marc No. 25 are in the historic style, with capitals as conglomerations patterned on the Grecian column orders, and the leap in style is, therefore, great next to that of another office building, that at rue Reamur No. 124, which is only 10 years younger.

In rue Reamur, annual architect competitions were held before and after the turn of the century, and these resulted in the street becoming one of the most interesting for studying the architecture of single buildings at the fin-de-siecle in Paris. No. 124 was erected for the newspaper Le Parisien Liberé in 1904–1905 and is commonly ascribed to the architect Georges Chedanne (1861–1940). The uncertainty concerning its designer stems from the fact that the drawings that remain for this address, dated 1903, do not correspond at all to the building that was erected. Chedanne was a significant architect with both national and international commissions, but nothing he designed either before or after has any particular relationship to the unique building at rue Reamur No. 124. The explanation may be that Chedanne delegated responsibility for this building to a needy colleague, while he himself concentrated on his other commissions, which probably were more prestigious.[7]

Regardless of the identity of its designer, rue Reamur No. 124 represents a breakthrough. All at once, the facade became a pure study in steel and glass. Bundles of columns appear to grow out of the ground and reach out to the bay windows at cornice height. The allusion to organic plant forms in the prevailing Art Nouveau style is obvious. Like trees, the columns surge out of the life of the facades and hold the bay windows, which with their reflections in the glass appear like heavy treetops. On their way, the columns hold powerful steel plate girders that mark floor divisions and serve as horizontal facade divisions. The entrance appears where two columns swing in to merge with the others in the column bundle. Thus, the opening is created by pushing the bearing structures to the sides.

No. 124 represents the entry to a new century and a new age. With its almost feminine lines, it also points to steel's many form manifestations. Fifty years before the big buildings of the Mies van der Rohe school, we have here steel's plastic properties displayed for what they are—not as copies of classical stone architecture—and steel in unison with glass as a total, formal, and structural means of expression.

*Right: Office building
on rue St. Marc, Paris,
1894
Architect: L.
Thalheimer*

*Below: Le Parisien
Liberé
View from the entrance*

STEEL, THE PROCESS
AND THE PRODUCT

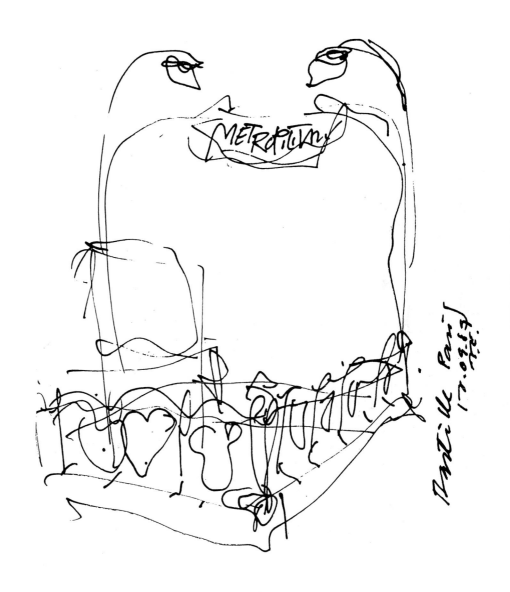

Metro entrance, La
Bastille, 1900
Architect: Hector
Guimard

From Iron Ore to Rolled Sections

Most steel is 98% to 99% iron, Fe (ferrum), the remainder being primarily carbon (C), silica (Si), manganese (Mn), chromium (Cr), and nickel (Ni). Impurities like sulfur (S), phosphorus (P), and nitrogen (N) must be eliminated. While there is no accepted international definition for steel, it is understood to be a molten iron product containing varying amounts of carbon (up to 1.7 %) that without further treatment is malleable, i.e., can be shaped in a warm but firm state.

Steel can be divided into three classifications: non-alloy, low-alloy, and alloy steel. Alloy steel is steel to which significant amounts of other metals have been added in sufficient quantities so as to produce clearly identifiable new properties in the material. Stainless steel, for example, may contain up to 20 weight percent of chromium and nickel. Non-alloy steel, or so-called carbon steel, is steel with properties determined to a large extent by its carbon content. Common construction steel is a non-alloy steel with a carbon content of approximately 0.2 weight percent. Manganese may be present up to 1.5 %, and also small amounts of phosphorus, sulfur, and nitrogen. Low-alloy steel is identical to regular construction steel except that it has somewhat greater amounts of manganese, chromium, and nickel to increase its strength and hardness, and possibly also copper to improve its resistance to corrosion. The amount of alloy that warrants the designation "non-alloy" or "low-alloy" will vary according to the individual alloying elements.

The English word "steel" originates from the Old English word *stele,* meaning firm, stiff, or inflexible.[8] Steel is the final product in a process that begins with the raw material in the form of iron ore, i.e., a rock or mineral with a high iron content. Let us briefly describe the most important stages in the production of steel, a process that transforms iron ore first to pig iron and later to steel.

Pig iron is produced in a blast furnace that is filled with layers of iron ore, coke, and lime. The blast furnace is an elevated, shaft-like combustion chamber lined with bricks. Before it is poured into the blast furnace, the iron ore is enriched, i.e., the most valuable minerals are concentrated by removal of the other minerals. This process of preparing the iron ore for smelting is also called beneficiation and consists of bringing the iron ore to a crushed or ground consistency suitable for pouring into the blast furnace. The coke, which serves as fuel for the smelting process in the blast furnace, is made from coal with the aid of a coke works. When warm air is added during combustion, the coke reacts with the oxygen to form carbon monoxide (CO) as it produces heat. The carbon monoxide reacts with the oxygen in the iron ore to form reduced iron and carbon dioxide (CO2). The melting point drops and the iron becomes fluid.

Lime is then added in the form of crushed limestone and combines with the rock part of the iron ore. This takes place in the fluid state, and the mixture—called slag—can be tapped from the blast furnace. The entire process is continuous, with ore, coke, and lime being poured in from the top of the furnace while warm air is being blown in from the bottom. The layers of material gradually seep down to the bottom of the blast furnace where the temperature is higher. Thus melted pig iron collects at the bottom, covered by a layer of melted slag. These are tapped several times every 24 hours. To produce one ton of pig iron, you need two tons of iron ore, one ton of coke, and 250 kg of limestone.

Pig iron from the blast furnace contains up to 10 % other elements, of which as much as 4 % is carbon. This iron is also called cast iron (see chapter 3). Producing steel is then a matter of refining the pig iron by removing the excess carbon and several other impurities and adding the desired alloying elements.

g iron being poured
to the converter at
e steelworks.

Steel production is accomplished by either of two principal methods: the converter process or the electric-furnace process. Briefly, the converter process involves oxidation of the undesired elements in the pig iron. Sir Henry Bessemer (1813–1898) is considered to have discovered the principle behind this method of steel production in 1856. It was further improved by S.G. Thomas in 1879. The most important converter process in use today is the LD method (Linz-Donawitz). This method removes impurities through oxidation, that is by blowing pure oxygen or oxygen-enriched air against the pig iron in the converter. The oxygen contains lime powder that can form a slag for binding non-gaseous impurities such as sulfur and phosphorus. The oxidation process removes, among other things, silicon, manganese, and nitrogen from the pig iron mass and lowers its carbon content from about 4 % to 0.1-0.2 %. Carbon is the most important alloying element and greatly affects the properties of steel. As the carbon content rises, steel's strength and hardness increase, while toughness and ductility decrease. The oxygen blowing technique makes the LD method easier to control than any other converter process, so that one can direct the input of ingredients more accurately, thereby facilitating a high degree of control of the quality of the steel. In the converter process the starting material is largely pig iron, but scrap iron can also be used.

The rolling mill

The electric furnace process, or electro-steel process, utilizes mainly scrap iron for steel production. Recycled iron and steel, and possibly also firm pig iron, are melted down in an electric furnace. Electro-steel receives a low content of phosphorus, sulfur, and nitrogen and has few slag components.

When the steel is ready in the electric-furnace it is tapped into ladles. There, additional refining takes place to lower the sulfur and phosphorus content even further. Also very important is the so-called deoxidation that removes unbound oxygen in the steel. This is so that it does not continue to react with the carbon. Locked-in oxygen creates pores in the steel. Gas formation can also cause roughness in the steel, which prevents it from being homogeneous, i.e., the distribution of carbon, sulfur, and phosphorus can be uneven. This condition is known as segregation. Porous steel with segregation is called rimmed steel.

The raw molten steel is lifted by ladle to the top of cast-iron molds, so-called strand casters, in order to form ingots. The ingots are laid in a soaking pit, and then processed in the roughing mill into slabs, blooms, or billets depending on the form of their cross-sections and their size. This is the first stage of steel formation before rolling.

Rolling aprons guide the steel to a roller leveler, where it is leveled and cut by torch into specific lengths. Then the steel forms proceed through the rolling mill. Several passes through a rolling mill shape the heated material into finished products. The resulting slabs are rolled into plates, sheets, and strips; the blooms into structural sections; and the billets into bars, rods, and tubes. These are the main groups of finished rolled products.

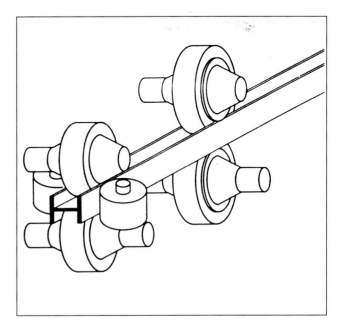

Rolling sections

Properties of Steel

Our discussion of the material properties of steel will be limited to its strength and stiffness, which along with its fire resistance, corrosion resistance, and the fact that it can be welded are the most relevant aspects of the material with regard to construction.

The way in which a soft-steel bar changes in length when subjected to stress can be graphically represented in a "stress-strain" diagram.[9] In accordance with Hooke's law, the diagram shows that the stress applied to a soft-steel bar is proportional to the strain experienced by the material up to a certain point referred to as "elastic limit." Up to this degree of stress, the steel bar retains its ability to go back to its original length once the load is removed. If the bar is subjected to stresses beyond this point, its deformation will be permanent. Soon after the elastic limit of the material is reached, the steel bar suddenly yields as it reaches the "yield point." After this initial sudden elongation the bar recovers the ability to resist increasing stress, but the percentage of elongation per unit of stress is much greater. This pattern continues up to a point at the top of the curve in the stress-strain diagram where the degree of stress finally reaches the "ultimate strength" of the material. After passing the point of ultimate strength, faster local failure occurs and the diameter of the bar decreases rapidly as it continues to elongate. The percentage of elongation may average about 30% and the reduction in cross sectional area is close to 50% at the point of rupture. These numbers indicate that soft-steel is a highly ductile material, a property that makes it a very desirable building material.

A simplified stress-strain diagram shows how soft steel behaves under stress before reaching permanent deformation.

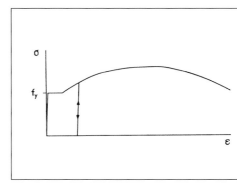

Hard steel has a higher carbon content, greater strength, and a higher elastic limit. It has no yield point but is more brittle, a property that makes it less desirable as a structural material since it would give little warning before failing.[10]

Steel's reliable strength and stiffness facilitate the precise calculation of its bearing capacity, which in turn allows for the material to be utilized economically in structures. The allowable stresses that are considered safe in each country are usually specified by their government agencies. These are published in codes available for reference to designers.

Whether steel can be welded is usually be determined by its carbon content. If common welding methods are used, the carbon content in the steel should be lower than about 0.5% to obtain a good result. An exception is wrought iron, which has a low carbon content but cannot be welded using modern methods.

Corrosion, or rusting, is an electrochemical process that deteriorates steel. In order for this to take place the steel must be exposed to water and oxygen as a thin layer of moisture on its surface. In the atmosphere practically no corrosion occurs when there is under 60% relative humidity. Therefore, steel does not rust indoors under dry conditions. From a relative humidity of 70% and up, corrosion occurs markedly with increasing humidity. Having access to air and water, corrosion will also greatly increase in a polluted industrial environment (which contains sulfur compounds or chlorides) and in sea water (salt). In contrast, clean air and very low temperatures (under 0° C / 32° F) will prevent the corrosion process considerably, so that an unpolluted mountain region will constitute a smaller corrosive threat than, for example, an industrial coastal region.

Resistance to corrosion varies with the type of steel. Common construction steel corrodes more quickly than most other steel varieties, but can be protected by galvanization or one or another form of paint treatment (see separate section on "Surface Treatment and Corrosion Protection").

Steel loses its strength and stiffness at high temperatures. At 400° C / 725° F steel has only two-thirds of its original strength and rigidity, and at 500° C / 900° F it retains only about half. Thereafter, the value sinks fast. As steel structures are usually light, with thin cross-sections, and possessing high thermal conductivity, entire structures can be heated quickly. The temperature of fire during its flame phase is normally 900–1,000° C. Therefore, a prolonged exposure to fire causes the temperature of a steel building to increase and the bearing capacity of its structure to drop dramatically.

When designing a steel structure, fire can be treated as a load in the same way a static loads, because the fire load, i.e., the amount of flammable material in th building and its heat value, is determinable. For a structure with a known use an form, therefore, the temperature development can be calculated with a high degre of accuracy, and comparisons can be made with the structure's heat resistance.

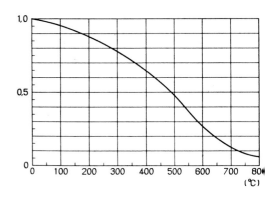

Reduction factor for steel's stiffness at high temperatures

Normally it is the building authorities who establish fire ratings for the constructic of various building types, but builders and insurance companies can also help i formulating regulations. Fire ratings are often expressed in minutes and hours burn time before the temperature in a building reaches a critical value, and ste structures are designed with the necessary fireproofing to meet the requiremen established by fire codes. The most common ways of fireproofing steel members a to coat them with antiflammable paint or some form of fire insulating foam, or encase them in concrete, hollow clay or terra cotta tile, gypsum or plaster. One m also consider oversizing the members to offer more resistance to fire. The choice method depends on the fire requirements and on budget considerations.

Table of material properties for a number of steel types

	Carbon steel (construction steel)	Low-alloyed steel	Cast steel	Wrought iron	Gray cast iron
Carbon content Weight %	0.15 - 0.20	0.20 - 0.25	0.50 - 1.50	0.05 - 0.10	2.5 - 4.0
Density (kg/dm³)	7.8	7.8	7.8	7.6	7.2
Surface tension*	230 - 300	340 - 450	200 - 400	180 - 200	
Breaking tension [or fracture tension]	350 - 550	400 - 700	400 - 600	300 - 350	150 - 350
Breaking [or fracture] lengthening (Ductility)	15 - 25	15	15 - 20	8 - 25	2
Elasticity module	$2.1 - 10^5$	$2.1 - 10^5$	$2.1 - 10^5$	$1.9 - 10^5$	$2.1 - 10^5$
Coefficient of heat development	$1.2 - 10^{-5}$	$1.2 - 10^{-5}$	$1.2 - 10^{-5}$	$1.2 - 10^{-5}$	$1.2 - 10^{-5}$
Weldability	good	good with the right alloys	moderate to good	as a rule, poor	poor
Corrosion resistance	poor	good with the right alloys	moderate	good	good
Temperature that gives 50% reduction in firmness	500	500	500	500	can crack at high temperatures

*or tension at 0.2% stretching

36

Structural Elements

Continuous casting, a method used to transform molten steel into finished forms, is the most widely used method of steel production. Very simply, the rolled products can be divided into sections and plates. Sections are heat rolled, formed in the red-hot state, whereas plates can be hot- or cold-rolled. Cold rolling can be done at room temperature.

Hot-rolled structural-steel shapes include bars, plates, and angles. These shapes are designed primarily to withstand tension forces. Other types of structural-steel shapes like W, S, and M, as well as many variations of steel channels, are designed primarily to withstand compression and bending, such as in columns and beams. When shapes are rolled, the molten steel passes through rollers that form it into the appropriate profiles. The shapes are delivered in standard lengths but can also be ordered in custom-cut lengths.

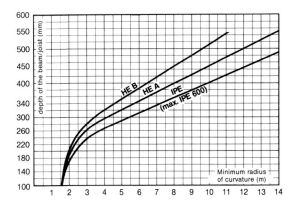

Minimum radius of bending curvature in meters of several section types.

Plate products are divided into thick, medium, and thin plates. Thick plates are 5 mm / 2" or more in thickness, while the medium plates are 3-5 mm / 1¼ to 2". These are also called bearing plates. Plates with thicknesses under 3 mm / 1¼" are called thin plates. Thick and medium plates are used frequently in welded beams, while thin plates are used more often in the manufacture of a wide range of products, such as thin-plate sections. After milling, the plates come out as rolls or coils and are cut into standard lengths, or they continue to cold milling. In order to give the plates the same material properties throughout their entire cross section, the heat treatment can take place during the cold milling itself. Cold milling allows for thinner dimensions, better pressure tolerances, and more precise surfaces than warm milling.

37

Facing page:
Production of
castellated beams with
the help of digital blow
torches at Westok
Structural Services,
Ltd., Wakfield,
England.

Expanded metal is a steel product in the form of a grid or grille that is made by slitting and subsequently stretching a steel plate. Expanded metal is mechanically produced—the steel plate is systematically slit and stretched by a machine.

Perforated plates are also mechanically fabricated by stamping out the steel plate. Perforated plates have a great number of applications, and they are also produced in aluminum and brass. Expanded metal and perforated plates have traditionally been used in industrial products such as protective grills, safety nets, steps, and foot bridges. Architects have come to accept them and often use them in their work. The transparency and light weight of these plates, as well as the rich possibilities for variation of perforation and slitting patterns, have helped them gain entry in new areas—paneled ceilings, facades, parapets, and the like.

Built-up steel beams and girders can be custom-designed for different and specific structural purposes. Although these are not off-the-shelf products, the most often used structural sections can generally be special-ordered with a short delivery time. Welded plate girders, so called built-up plate girders, are often used in bridge construction.

Federal Center,
Chicago, 1973
Architect: Mies van der
Rohe
The precision of steel
expressed with
standard sections.

Steel trusses are commonly used for large spans. These are constructed either with welded hot-rolled shapes—for example, using T-shapes as top and bottom chords and angles as diagonal members—or entirely built of welded tubular sections.

Castellated beams are made by cutting a W-beam or an S-beam longitudinally along the web in a straight or curved zigzag shape. The two halves of the beam are separated, displaced, and then welded together again. The final product is twice as deep as the original beam but not any heavier. With this procedure, then, the bearing capacity of the beam increases up to 100% without any increase in weight. Castellated beams are economical when they are industrially produced with fully automated blowtorches and welding machines.

Tubular steel is produced in circular as well as square and rectangular sections. Square and rectangular tubular sections are produced in many different sizes of varying wall thickness. Structurally, these sections respond very well to torsion forces and are therefore ideal as columns.

Tubes are produced in various ways and can be either hot- or cold-rolled. Tubes with seams, so-called welded tubes, are made of plates shaped into a cylinder and joined by a long weld where the ends meet. Another variation is to shape the plate into a spiral that can be welded together. This method is well-suited for large diameters. Seamless pipes are produced from solid cylindrical or square sections that are pressed over a punch with a diameter similar to the desired diameter of the tube.

Corrugated steel sheets are formed from cold-milled sheets. Sheets are generally coated with zinc, aluminum, or both. They could also be painted, galvanized, ceramic coated, or plastic coated. Plastic coated sheets are always zinc-coated first. The size of a corrugated sheet is specified by its pitch and depth; its thickness by the gage. Pitch is measured from crown to crown of the corrugation, and depth from crown to valley. Corrugated steel is frequently used as siding or roofing in the construction of light prefabricated buildings, industrial sheds, and the like.

*toil's oil refinery,
ngstad
e steel has many
ns of expression.*

Pump factory,
Quimper, France, 1982
Main structure
showing the effective
utilization of steel pipes
and standard sections.
The facade is cladded
with silver anodized
corrugated steel.
Architect: Richard
Rogers & Partners
Engineers: Ove Arup &
Partners

Joining Methods

Steel members are joined either by welding or bolting. Riveted joints, which once were commonly used, are now less common. Today they are mainly used in lap joints.

Deciding whether a connection should be welded or bolted depends on a number of factors. One factor that must be taken into account is the project's structural concept, which is based on sound knowledge of the materials and how this knowledge should be applied. One must determine whether the construction of the entire structure or just parts of it will be carried out at the shop. When assembly is done at the building site, a great deal of preparatory work will always have to be done in the shop. There, welding will be the most economical method of obtaining strong connections. At the building site, elements will usually be assembled by bolting, mainly because it is quicker, easier, and cheaper. Cranes and other transport equipment are very costly, and it is important not to delay other aspects of the construction. Another factor to be reckoned with is the surface treatment of the steel. It is best to bolt together elements that have been surface coated. Welding together members that have been galvanized or painted should be avoided.

Pin welding at the job site.

Since the 1940s, welding has developed rapidly to overwhelmingly become the most common method of joining steel. The term "welding" means the melting together of two members, or steel parts, so that an unbroken connection is achieved along the fusing edges, as well as a homogeneous continuity of the fused members. During welding, steel in the welding zone melts, creating a fusion when it cools between the two surfaces themselves or between these surfaces and a filler material.

During welding the steel in the welding zone melts very quickly. The material in and surrounding the completed weld is affected to different degrees, and can be divided into different zones that have a different physical structure. In these different zones, mechanical tensions occur that attempt to dislodge the welded parts. The welder must master these conditions in order to do a proper job.

Methods of joining metal parts together have been used for thousands of years. In Egyptian pharaoh tombs drinking vessels were found with handles soldered fast with silver. The development of the welding methods used today began at the end of the last century with the invention of electric-arc welding. The arc was so strong that the material's welding joint melted. The first electrodes to be used were of carbon, and later of metal. The problem with these methods was that they didn't keep out oxygen, which led to brittleness and impurities in the weld.

Early this century, the Swede Oskar Kjellberg developed the coated-electrode in use today. It has a covering outside the filler material that melts with the heat of the arc and forms a gaseous shield that prevents oxygen and nitrogen from coming in contact with the molten pool. Gas welding was developed about the same time as electric-arc welding. With a flame produced by a burning mixture of acetylene and oxygen, the temperature becomes sufficiently hot to weld steel. Manual welding is the most common method of welding for smaller tasks. For longer projects, the automatic welding methods are most economical and, therefore, in most widespread use.

Centre Le Corbusier,
Zurich, 1967
Typical frame corner
with bolted connections
Architect: Le Corbusier

Bolt connection requires bolts, nuts, and washers, and can be used in joining structural steel. Found in many standardized shapes and sizes, bolts are classified by strength grades. There are "unfinished" bolts used for general application and piping systems, and high-strength bolts used specially in connections of high strength structural steel members. On high-strength bolts, the strength grade is stamped onto the bolt's head. Bolts used in steel buildings are usually galvanized by a hot-dip zinc process to provide good corrosion resistance.

The selection and placement of bolts is important. In addition to securing a good connection, the washer may serve as a visual complement to the union.

44

GLAZED SPACES

Galleria Vittorio
Emanuele II, Milan,
1865–67
Architect: Guiseppe
Mengoni

Glazed Galleries of Nineteenth-Century Paris

"Have you noticed that a bit of heaven seen through two chimneys or rocks, through a cellar window or an archway, gives a deeper picture of infinity than the big panorama we see from a high mountain?"

—Charles Baudelaire

In his book *Paris, die Hauptstadt des XIX Jahrhunderts,* Walter Benjamin cites two important prerequisites for the appearance and development of the glazed streets, or galleries. The first is prosperity in the textile industry, which provided the economic basis for trade in many kinds of luxury items. The galleries, then, became a center for this trade. An illustrated guide to Paris from the time describes these "glass-covered, marble-clad pedestrian passages through entire city blocks" like this: "On each side of these passages, which get their light from above, are rows of the most elegant boutiques, so that, in other words, one can say that such a passage is a city, yes, a world, in miniature."[11] The second condition that made the galleries possible was the development of iron as a structural building material. Due to its properties, iron was able to bear glass roofs with a minimum of materials.

Passage du Caire,
Paris, 1799

The galleries in Paris were essentially built during the first half of the 19th century, with Passage du Caire from 1799 as the first and Passage Jouffroy from 1845 as the last large one. In the narrow skylit streets, the new enlightened bourgeoisie in Imperial Paris could wander among the display windows and shops full of luxury items without getting wet. With the exception of the Passage du Caire, the oldest of them all, the galleries became places where the well-to-do went to see and be seen, and to exchange money for goods. The galleries can be seen as the forerunners of large department stores.

As a building type the galleries occupy a unique position. The roofs, as pure structures of iron and glass, span from the second or third story of one brick commercial building to another, thereby forming a sheltered environment. In this respect, the roofs do not constitute an independent building as much as they are superstructures occupying the interstitial spaces created by two buildings, and contributing to the general character of these spaces as streetscapes. Varying in width between 3–5 m / 10 x 17', the linearity of the galleries is one of their predominant characteristics. The entrances are well-defined, often with triumphal-arch portals, leading us, as in a one-point perspective, to the next station point, marking a shift in direction along our linear course. This optical and physical movement creates a sense of infinity. The roof construction is repeated in similar sections and always conveys the same expression that reflects a serial, mechanical production.

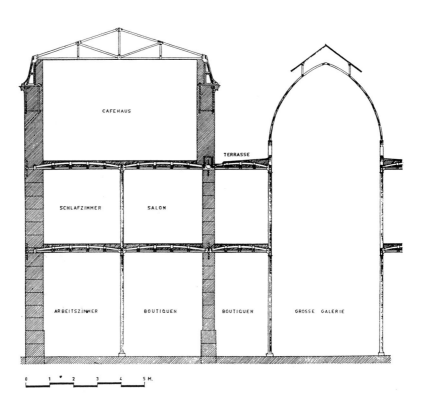

Passage Jouffroy,
Paris, 1845
Cross section of gallery
and side building

The short span does not really put iron to any decisive structural test. In principle any known roof form and truss geometry could be utilized, but most often we find barrel vaults and the simple gable roof. However, the structural nature of the cross section is not especially emphasized. Cross sections and longitudinal sections often have the same character, contributing to the lace-like character of the iron structures with uniform dimensions in the structural elements.

The gallery roofs, especially the earlier ones, are therefore devoid of any structural hierarchy that could emphasize the differences between the short cross span and the apparently endless spatial elongation. As a consequence, the iron and glass structures have, as a whole, more surface character than linear character, and are reminiscent of a kind of tent structure, or even of abstract masonry structures with glass stones.

In an attempt to trace the origins and inspirational sources of the galleries, we also encounter the Oriental bazaar. These were well known to tradesmen and warriors who had spent time in Arab countries of the Middle East and northern Africa. Their influence is obvious in the construction of Paris's oldest gallery, which was built immediately after Napoleon Bonaparte's Egyptian campaign in 1799, and was aptly named Passage du Caire. This gallery is 370 m / 1,225' long with an average width of only 2.7 m / 9'. The thin iron mullions between the glass panes in the gable roof butt up against the roof ridge section. Every fifth mullion is connected to a tension member that hangs from the roof ridge. The sections are reduced to minimum thickness, and at the gallery's pivot point the structure seems charmingly improvised and irregular. The fortuitous geometry that is created is silhouetted sharply against the sky as a rich graphic pattern of iron lines.

Passage Jouffroy (1845) is special in that the iron structure is continued right down to the ground and dictates the character of the inner space to a large degree. Between the slender, load bearing iron columns, the display windows open fully and form a new spatial arrangement that is later developed further in large department stores. The big attraction in this gallery is Musée Grevin, the Parisian counterpart to Madame Tussaud's wax museum in London. The iron and glass roof connects the two sides of the gallery over a span of 4.6 m /15' using a barrel vault form. The curved mullions bear the glass panes and rest on two T-shaped purlins running lengthwise. Every eighth mullion extends to the top of the vault and screws to the one opposite, thus providing support for the longitudinal purlins. Atop the vault is a gabled ventilation hood that runs longitudinally and rests on the purlins. Passage Jouffroy's very slender, elegant iron structure outlines the contour of the entire space. In this way, Passage Jouffroy at once utilizes the influences of its precursors and constitutes the transition to other building types with completely independent iron structures.

Facing page: Passage Jouffroy, Paris, 1845

48

Kew and Kibble

The Royal Botanical Garden at Kew outside London is the English garden *pa* *excellence*. Of its several greenhouses we will discuss the Palm House (1848) designed by the architects Decimus Burton and Richard Turner. The Kew Palm House combines Loudon's principle of curved glass with Paxton's assertion that the technical qualities of a building should be expressed in new contemporary glass architecture.

The Royal Botanical Garden, Kew, Palm House, 1848 Architects: Decimus Burton and Richard Turner

The design is based on a combination of pure geometric shapes. The glass skin is stretched over the structural frame, which consists of arched cast iron ribs in a light 3.75 m / 12'4" module. The ribs are connected with horizontal stays. In the central space, the other ribs are supported by columns and corbels of cast iron. The corbels, which are double, shore up the frame construction and provide support for the interior gallery.

Today, a walk up the beautiful spiral staircase to the gallery where the entire greenhouse has been thoroughly restored—and where the tropical rain forest vegetation has still not gained dominance—reveals white-painted cast iron and glass in 30° C / 86°F heat and 100% relative humidity. The lightness and elegance of the space stems from its technical virtuosity.

Kibble Palace (1872), in the botanical gardens in Glasgow, is a late zenith in the development of iron and glass filigree work. The idea of a crystal palace—covering a space entirely with glass—is here taken to its extreme conclusion by John Kibble, architect, engineer, and innovator. The splendid glass dome with a diameter of

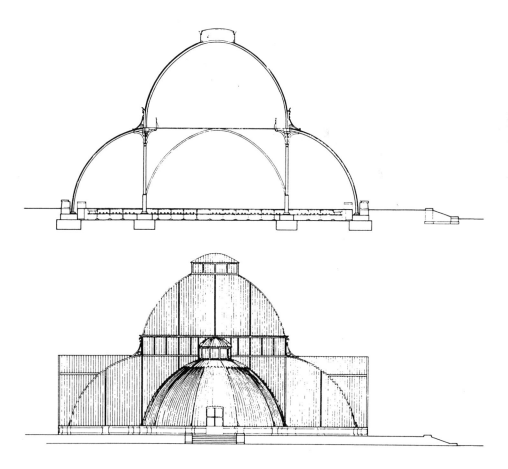

The Royal Botanical Garden, Kew, Palm House, 1848 Cross section and elevation

44.5 m / 147' is particularly well worth closer study. The dome is supported by two perimeter beams that form two concentric compression rings supported, respectively, by 12 and 24 cast iron columns. The slender columns are cast and detailed with spiral fluting. The connection between the column and the perimeter beam is beautifully facilitated by a small Corinthian capital and, above, two triangular filigree plates that elegantly, yet effectively prevent the dome from twisting from torsion.

In the greenhouse in Kew, the iron ribs are placed at a large distance from one another—3.75 m / 12'4". In Kibble Palace, the ribs are placed closely together, are more slender, and also serve as mullions for the glass. The ribs rest on the above mentioned compression rings, defining the shape of the dome.

Kibble understood how to use and further develop the best work of his predecessors. Loudon's principle of the curved glass panes was fully applied. The building's 100th anniversary in 1972 also celebrated its exceptional durability and technical perfection. Kibble Palace still stands today and is well-maintained.

Botanic Gardens,
Glasgow, Kibble
Palace, 1872
Architect and engineer:
James Kibble

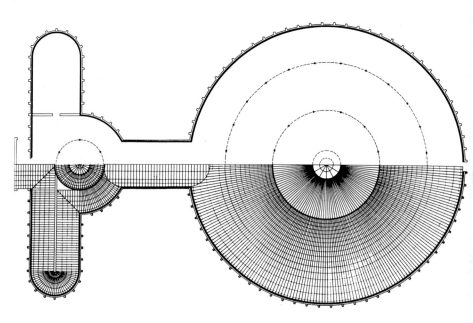

otanic Gardens,
lasgow, Kibble
alace, 1872
rchitect and engineer:
mes Kibble

The Galleria Vittorio Emanuele II in Milan

As mentioned in the preceding section, glass-covered streets have their origin in the Parisian gallery. This type of structure was established and acknowledged in the 1860s as an important planning element in many European city centers. Geist has described more than 300 such structures from the 19th century in his work on glass galleries alone.[12]

The Galleria Vittorio Emanuele II in Milan (1865–67), by architect Guiseppe Mengoni, is undoubtedly the most splendid example of them all. Here, the building type reaches its full monumental expression. It unites Piazza del Duomo with Piazza della Scala, as well as two secondary streets on each side. The complex encompasses four blocks in which the two intersecting passages are defined by glazed barrel vaults. The point of intersection is defined by a central dome with a span of 36.6 m / 121', the same dimension as the dome of St. Peter's Church in Rome. The 14.5 meter- / 48 foot-wide passages are flanked by richly detailed stone facades in a taut rhythmic order. The ribbed vaults are refreshingly simple and elegantly executed as arched trusses without diagonal members. The buildings on either side receive the lateral thrust so that there is no need for tension stays. A ventilation hood runs centrally above the arches, along the barrel vault. The dome, whose structural frame is similar to the one in the barrel vaults, is crowned by a lantern. On the ground level there are shops, cafes, and restaurants; offices and studios are on the third floor. The floors above these are, surprisingly, apartments that can be reached from the courtyard outside the gallery.

It is important to note that this complex is planned as a whole. There is a consistency between the buildings' stone character and the light steel-and-glass roofs, and a clarity in the difficult connection between vault and dome. The plan's success stems from the original architectural concept—a concept that is also reflected in the polished, multicolored geometrical patterns of the stone floor.

The gallery provides a majestic stage set for the swarming everyday life between two of Milan's most significant institutions: the Gothic cathedral in Piazza del Duomo and La Scala, perhaps the world's most famous opera house. The gallery is open because of the mild climate.

Galleria Vittorio
Emanuele II, Milan,
1867
Architect: Guiseppe
Mengoni

Gallertia Vittorio Emanuele II, Milan, 1867
Artist Saul Steinberg's impression of daily activities in Milan's famous gallery.

The University Center in Trondheim

The competition for a new university center in Trondheim, Norway, was announced in 1968. After two submission rounds, the Danish architect Henning Larsen was declared the winner. The idea behind the winning proposal was to create a tight urban structure consisting of three-story blocks with glass-covered streets between them. Areas of communal functions, such as auditoriums, the student association, shops, etc., were placed on the ground level. This was done not only to encourage traffic on the streets, but to also encourage informal gatherings and conversation— in short, to encourage the very activity that defines an urban society. As we have seen in preceding sections, this is not a new idea, but rather a modern interpretation of the great glazed galleries of nineteenth-century London, Paris, and Milan.

The building complex, which is planned based on a strict module and measures 8.4 x 8.4 m / 28 x 28' with a height of 3.5 m / 12', was erected with a widespread use of prefabricated concrete components—in principle a two-way column and beam system. Connecting bridges, elevator shafts, and overhead lighting structures are done in heat-galvanized steel.

From early sketches one can see that the glass roof covering the street was originally vaulted. With such notable models as the Galleria Vittorio Emanuele II in Milan, this is not so surprising. However, the arched shape was abandoned in favor of a gabled roof, reportedly because no supplier would guarantee the uppermost glass pane, which was horizontal.

The solution that was realized is based on steel trusses with a triangular cross section that spans the width of the street, 8.4 m / 28', the dimension of the module. The sloping glass panes rest on horizontal side purlins in steel, which in turn are connected to the top chord of the trusses. The choice of tubular sections for the side purlins is worth noting. Circular tubular sections can take loads from all sides, in contrast to the typical I-beams, which are designed to withstand loads along a single axis.

The glass-covered streets afford the university complex its special character, partially because of the street activities and partially due to the background views of the Trondelag countryside and the fjord.

The climate in the gallery is excellent. In the winter months the temperature in the gallery is usually maintained with the help of surplus heat from the enclosing buildings. Summer temperatures are also comfortable since excess heat from the sun is released through vents in the uppermost parts of the glazed roof. In addition should there ever be a fire, the roof can be "opened" to allow the smoke to escape. The project has contributed a great deal to the expensive research being carried on at the University Center.

The University Center,
Trondheim
Detail of the street
intersection
Architect: Henning
Larsen

The University Center,
Trondheim
Glazed street
Architect: Henning
Larsen

The Glass Pyramids in Paris

Born in 1917, architect Ieoh Ming Pei's pyramid in Paris resembles the top of a huge iceberg. As the first phase in the major reorganization and expansion of the Louvre, the construction of the pyramid has enabled the institution to maintain its standing among the largest and most beautiful museums in the world. Besides providing the museum's formidable new vestibule with daylight, the pyramid underscores the beginning of the Louvre-La Defense axis. At a height of 21.5 m / 72' and with 35 m /118' sides, the glass pyramid stands like an elegantly polished diamond in the Cour Napoleon, surrounded by the museum's 18th-century stone buildings. What makes the pyramid—with its cladding of 612 rhombus-shaped glass panels—stand requires more careful examination.

Each surface of the pyramid consists of 32 intersecting trusses of different lengths lying parallel to the edge of the surface. The trusses' compression member, primarily the top chord and the perpendicular chords, are built of circular tubular sections, while the tension members, the bottom, and diagonal chords are solid rods or cables. The glass panes are fastened at the intersecting points of the top chords by means of extension bolts, so that they are connected to the structural system but free from bearing any loads.

Suction on the glass surface is achieved by another method. Sixteen tension cables, or counter cables, connect the joints along the bottom chord of the trusses and hold the entire structure together.

The pyramid's structure lies within the French tradition that begins with Polonceau's achievements in the 19th-century, incorporating subtle variations between compression and tension components in steel structures. The key to the pyramid's bearing system lies, however, in the cast stainless steel joints. The turnbuckle and clevis used in the system come from the riggings of sailboats and yachts. These are minimal structures designed exclusively to withstand tension in the same way as they function on a boat's rigging, to stiffen the masts with tension cables. With the help of outstanding "seamanship," then, it was possible to succeed in rigging and stiffening all the joints beneath the pyramid's precise glass surfaces.

The inverted pyramid, Pyramide Inversée, designed in 1993 by architect I.M. Pe
and engineer Peter Rice, works as a skylight for the underground galleries :
Carrousel. This pyramid, too, falls along the Louvre-La Defense axis. The inverte
pyramid points downward with a 13.3 x 13.3-meter / 45 x 45-foot base at groun
level and an apex that is just 1.4 m/ 4½' above the gallery floor.

The pyramid shape, with its slanted glass surfaces, contributes to maximize the flo
of daylight into the galleries. The inverted form of this pyramid called for a differei
structural solution, one that consists of two independent parts: a lower, inverte
pyramid and an upper, almost flat pyramid which is stabilized by its own weight an
protects the inverted one from wind loads.

Unlike the main pyramid, in which the glass panes are mounted on aluminu
mullions, the glass surfaces of the inverted pyramid have no mullions, following tl
principles of structural glass construction. The 112 rhombus-shaped glass pan
are joined at the corners by small cruciform fittings in cast stainless steel attache
to joints inserted in the glass. The internal structure consists of a system of sta
that prevents the diagonally suspended surfaces from buckling outward. Fi
vertical layers of cables thereby connect the cruciform fittings in the glass surfac
to "flying rods" suspended from a perimeter beam. This construction was original
developed by R. Buckminster Fuller in the 1950s.

Of note is that the pyramid hangs indoors so that there are no wind loads on i
surfaces, neither pressure nor suction. So far, the Pyramide Inversée is the late
step in the very rapid development of structural glass construction.

Grev Wedel's Place 9 in Oslo

Office building at Grev Wedel's Place 9, Oslo, 1992
Middle courtyard with glass roof
Architect: LPO Architect Office, Inc.
Engineer: Groner, Inc.

Over the central courtyard of this office building, which also contains the Astrup Fearnley Art Museum, is an outspread structure of steel and glass that is about the lightest and most delicate that can be built today. The idea for the vaulted roof came from the building's architects, the LPO Architect Office, and has been refined and developed from their original winning entry to the competition held in 1989, and still further to the light roof that was finally built in compliance with the builder's recommendations. Important supporters of the project have also been the Ove Arup engineering office in London and, later, the Groner engineering firm, which modified the structure and completed the calculations.

The most characteristic visual feature of the structure is the equal size of the steel sections in both spanning directions. In other words, the roof is a structural grid that does not present a hierarchy of primary and secondary structural elements. Visually, the result is a transparent membrane or shell that does not lead the eye in any definite direction, but that gives the illusion of a net that is stretched over the roof opening.

The visual lightness of the roof cover is the result of the complex structural system. The roof structure can be characterized as a shell built of a square grid of glass panes 1.35 x 1.35 m / 4½ x 4½' in size. The mullions are tubular sections measuring 100 x 50 mm / 4 x 2" and are welded together—a very delicate structure for a vaulted roof spanning 13.5 m/ 45'. These small dimensions are possible because the tubular sections act jointly with 12 mm / $^{15}\!/_{32}$" steel wires fastened to each intersection, running in a diagonal grid over the entire roof surface. The wires are galvanized and anchored with stainless steel joints in the form of plates that clamp the wires to the junctures in both directions. The steel wires are key elements in this structural system, working in tension against the downward bending in parts of the roof surface, and in compression counteracting the tendency to lift upward in other parts. With their help, the loads on the roof surface are distributed evenly over the entire shell in both the diagonal and the orthogonal directions. Each wire has a prestressed strength of 10kN.

At each end of the roof there are steel trusses which receive the loads from the wires. There are also steel trusses running longitudinally along both long sides of the roof that receive the lateral thrust from the vault and tension forces from the wires. These are not visible, and are mutually united by a tension cable that runs along the entire perimeter of the roof cover and receives the horizontal roof loads. These steel trusses lie horizontally to maintain the visual transparency of the roof surface.

The glass lies directly on the steel structure, a so-called planar system, from the glass producer, Pilkington. The glass panes are in two layers, with tempered glass on top, and are bolted to each juncture in the structural grid by means of a cruciform steel plate. The two layers of glass are joined by silicon, a solution Pilkington guarantees will remain sealed at temperatures down to 2° C / 35° F.

The dimensioning criteria for the structure were set to minimize deformation. The roof is so rigid that there is a maximum displacement of 2 degrees of angular change between each pane in the grid. Such stiffness guarantees that the glass joints will remain tightly sealed. An interesting aspect of this glass system is that even though the cost per square meter is higher than for a conventional solution, the final cost will be competitive because this system saves on the total number of square meters of glass. Conventional glass-roof solutions normally require at least a drop of 28 degrees,

which prompts one to build gable roofs, semicircular roofs, and other variations th
require a greater glass surface over the same span. Moreover, these glazing syste
afford the architect a greater degree of freedom and flexibility in design, allowing t
final product to be as close as possible to the original idea. Minimized glazing syste
such as this one combined with extraordinary bearing properties of steel bring gl
roofs still closer to the utopian ideal of complete transparency.

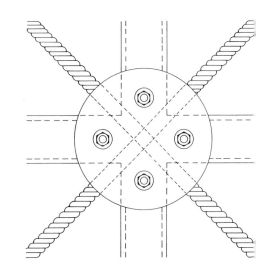

*Office building at Grev
Wedel's Place 9, Oslo,
1992
Detail of wire
moorings seen from
below.*

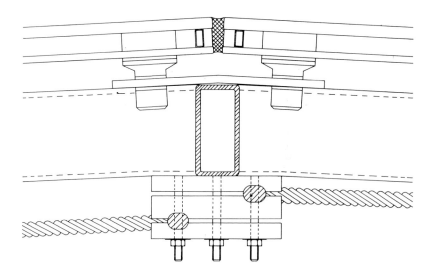

*Office building at Grev
Wedel's Place 9, Oslo,
1992
Detail section of wire
mooring, steel section,
and glass structure.*

Forge and Cast Iron and Steel

Material Properties

Iron reacts very easily with oxygen. This is why the iron we find in nature is in the form of iron oxides, compounds of iron, and oxygen. An important task in the production of iron for utility objects is to remove the oxygen in the compound. This is done by heating iron oxide together with carbon, which is found in charcoal, coke, or limestone, because the carbon reacts even more easily with oxygen that iron does. Thereby the iron oxide is reduced, i.e., it releases oxygen, by the carbon uniting with the oxygen in the air to form carbon monoxide. This gas reacts with iron oxide to form reduced iron and carbon dioxide.

Porte Dauphine metro station, Paris, 1898 Architect: Hector Guimard

After this process, however, there is still some remaining carbon in the iron clump. This iron is called pig iron, or cast iron, and can be further converted into wrought iron by adding new oxygen and gradually reducing the carbon content in the cast iron.

Iron as a usable metal is in every instance an iron-carbon compound in which the carbon occurs in varying amounts. Even if the amount of carbon in relation to iron is small—measured in percentage of weight—because of the difference in its own weight the volume amount of carbon is, as a rule, considerable. This affects the metal's microstructure, i.e., the shape and size of the molecules, and gives the iron its most important properties.

As a utilized material wrought iron is definitely the oldest iron product, recorded in history for at least 4000 years. It is also the purest iron that can be used practically, in other words, the iron with the lowest amount of other substances. (For example, its carbon content can be less than 0.1% by weight.) Wrought iron has a fiber structure not unlike wood in its character, and has good tensile-strength properties. The material can be worked by hammering, pulling, or milling in the molten state. In this state, two pieces of wrought iron can also be joined by melting them together—a process that blacksmiths depended on. In architectural terms, wrought iron is only of historic interest, a point discussed later in the chapter.

Cast iron, first produced in the 1400s, is characterized by its high carbon content, usually 2.5-4.0%. This makes for an often brittle iron with a crystalline structure. The iron is easily shaped during casting, generally in molds of sand because it becomes fluid when heated. Cast iron withstands pressure well but can resist only light tensile stress. Its high carbon content, however, is the reason it is significantly more resistant to corrosion than wrought iron.

The most common types of cast iron are the gray and graphite-pellet cast irons. Gray cast iron is the traditional cast iron, in which the carbon is primarily found as graphite in flake form. The name refers to the iron's gray or grayish black color of its broken surfaces. Gray cast iron is a relatively brittle material because of the graphite flakes, and it has compression strength commonly three to five times that of its tensile strength.

Graphite-pellet cast iron is treated with magnesium in the molten state, which results in pellet-shaped graphite formations. A tendency toward cracking is attributable to the magnesium, yet the magnesium also makes the iron considerably stronger than gray cast iron. Therefore, pellet cast iron is a more ductile material than the traditional gray cast iron, i.e., it has plastic properties that make the material permanently deformed when overloaded, and it is not brittle. This is a very

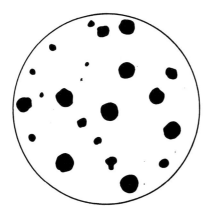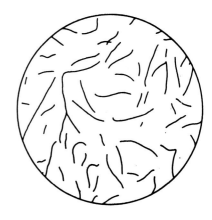

...hematic enlargement
... two types of cast
...on.
...ight: Gray cast iron
...ith graphite flakes.
...ft: Graphite pellet
...st iron.

important property when it comes to using cast iron in construction, especially in situations where the cast iron element is exposed to tensile or bending stress. Graphite-pellet cast iron is a relatively new material that was developed in the late 1940s, and with its ductile and strength properties it resembles steel more closely than gray cast iron. With great strength, ductility, and good castability, it combines three important properties in one material, making it an interesting choice architecturally. However, graphite-pellet cast iron cannot be welded.

Cast steel is an alloy with a higher manganese (Mn) and silicon (Si) content than comparable milled construction steel. What is more, the carbon content is considerably higher, approximately 0.5–1.5%. Manganese and silicon make the steel easier to cast and also cause oxygen to unite in such a way that there is no pore formation. Cast steel must be completely dense, (without porous substances) so that the material becomes as homogeneous as possible. In order to increase its mechanical strength, all cast steel is heat-treated before delivery. Cast steel is made in several qualities, and the best ones have stiffness properties and ductility that compare with milled construction steel. Particularly noteworthy vis-à-vis architecture, cast-steel can be welded, either to itself or to milled steel, so that combined constructions can be created.

Iron in Architecture

Throughout the Middle Ages, wrought iron was used increasingly in architecture fo
railings and gates. We can find wrought iron used in France for structural purpose
around 1670 when architect Claude Perrault (1613–1688) built the east facade o
the Louvre. Perrault used cast iron as a reinforcement for the brick structures tha
compose the entablature of the colonnade. Later, architect Germain Souffle
(1713–1780) and engineer Jean Rondelet (1734–1823) refined this technique whe
building the large columned vestibule for the Pantheon in Paris (1770). Toward th
end of the 1700s came the first independent wrought iron structures, around th
same time as smaller wrought and milled beam sections became available
Applications can be seen in many glass galleries, built from about 1800 forward, i
Paris and other European cities.

Cast iron had little place in architecture until the 1700s, and was used mostly i
decorated fireplace plates and similar objects in the household. Early in th
century, Christopher Wren (1632–1723) used cast iron in the guardrail around S
Paul's Cathedral in London, and was the pioneer in the structural use of cast iron i

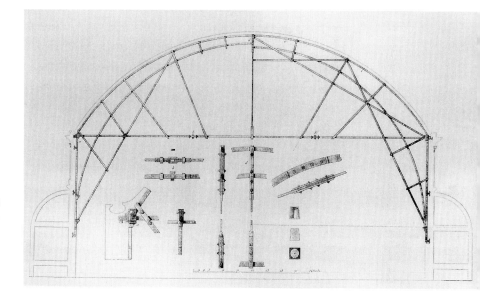

*Wrought-iron roof-truss
suggestions for Théâtre
Français, Paris, c.
1780*
*The left solution was
built.*

68

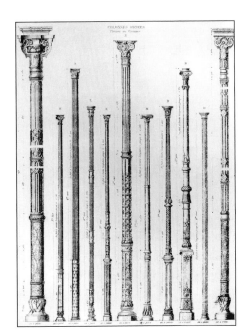

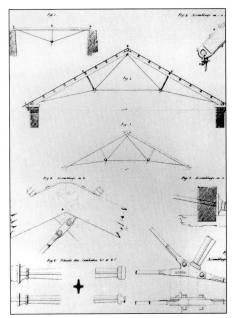

the slender iron columns that bear one of the galleries in the British Lower House. A breakthrough in the production and use of cast iron was reached in 1779 with the construction of Ironbridge at Coalbrookdale in England (see page 220).

The malleability and high tensile strength of wrought iron, and the brittle nature and high compression strength of cast iron, account for the different practical applications of both. Quite naturally, wrought iron was most preferably used in structures to withstand tensile forces and bending action, such as in pure tension members and beams, while cast iron was used to withstand compressive strain, such as in columns and arched structures. Larger, free-spanning structures of iron—in the decades leading up to the Crystal Palace, in 1851—were principally done as arched cast-iron structures. As the need for larger spans increased, engineers developed new construction techniques and principles. Among these were the stave structures or trusses in which wrought iron and cast iron, respectively, were used for tension and compression in one and the same structure. A good example of this is the Polonceau roof truss of the engineer, Camille Polonceau (1813–1859), which utilizes king post trusses with wrought iron beams and ties while the post, taking pure compression, are made of cast iron. In many ways, cast iron is easier to form. This can often be seen in the detailing of structural parts made out of cast iron, which makes the material easily identifiable.

In the latter half of the 19th century, cast iron was used less and less frequently in bearing structures that could be subjected to bending, except in relatively short spans. As steel made inroads, cast iron in columnar structures and pure compression disappeared. By then wrought iron's days were also numbered.

Cast Steel: New Architectonic Possibilities

During the last few decades, cast iron/carbon alloys have again found an application in architecture. Modern cast steel has properties that combine malleability with great strength and provide hitherto unknown possibilities of forming bearing structures. The formal possibilities are almost unlimited, but all shapes are not equally economical. A good design rule is that the cast piece should have soft, rounded shapes with a hollow groove in the transition between two directions, so as to reduce casting tensions and tensions that arise during the loading of the cast piece.

The breakthrough for cast steel in architecture came with the Centre Georges Pompidou in Paris (1977), by architects Richard Rogers (born 1933) and Renzo Piano (born 1937) and the engineering firm of Ove Arup & Partners. The building's principal structure consists of huge trusses about 45 m / 150' long, which span

Centre Pompidou, Paris, 1977
Architects: Renzo Piano and Richard Rogers
Engineer: Ove Arup & Partners

70

between the columns of each long facade. To counteract the one-sided load on the columns, there are cantilevered bracket projections mounted on them, so-called gerberettes, which, with the help of prestressed vertical stays, elicit an equal but opposite action on the columns. Ideally, the final result is moment-free columns without large tensile stress, but with extra compressive stress added. Many of the important parts of this system are done in cast steel. Cast steel pieces solve a complex connection of multiple tubular sections in the trusses and have a shape that only is attainable by casting. The gerberettes are similarly form casted, with soft lines and no sharp edges. The columns, with an outside diameter of 850 mm / 33 $7/16$" are cast by using a special centrifuging technique. The dimensions are minimized by striving for a pure compression load to avoid bending moments.

Centre Pompidou,
Paris, 1977
Steel montage

In addition to the elements in the main structure, cast steel is used in a number of other components, such as anchoring details and details related to the bracing system. This entire architectural masterpiece can be seen as a gigantic laboratory for the use of cast steel in architecture.

New applications for cast steel construction will presumably develop in the years to come. Complex structures that utilize cast components to a greater degree can be anticipated, as can more organic forms with soft transitions. This could mean shapes that are better suited to their tasks, which could also imply greater material efficiency. The relatively short production route from raw material to finished building part, and the possibilities for optimizing the material's strength with alloying and tempering, could make cast steel structures very cost-effective.

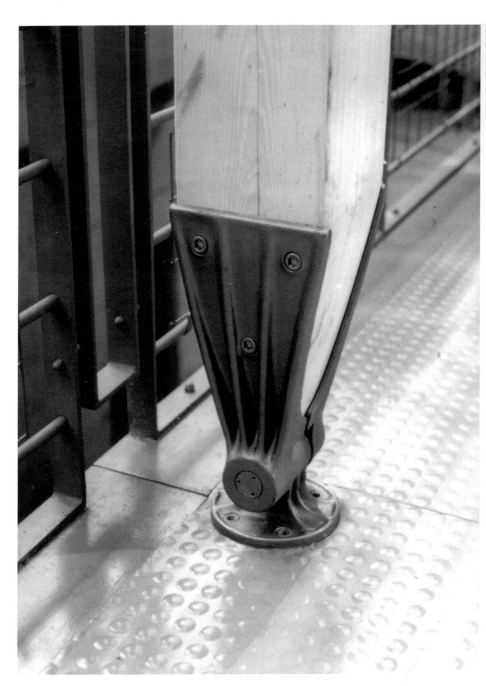

The Architecture School, Lyon, 1988 Cast-steel detail for wooden pillars Architects: Jourda and Perraudin Engineers: Rice, Francis, Ritchie

MULTI-STORY BUILDINGS

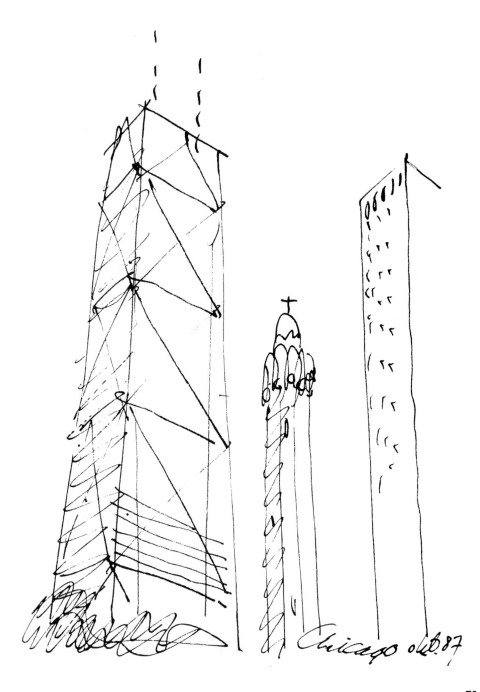

John Hancock Center,
Chicago, 1969
Architect: SOM
Engineer: Fazlur Khan

Structural Principles

Multi-storied buildings are buildings of several floors in which the floor height remains more or less constant as you proceed upwards, and in which this height is usually no more than 3–4 m / 10–13.3'. Thus, multi-storied buildings are office buildings, residential buildings, etc., anywhere from two floors high to high rises. Structurally, the approach to such buildings is frequently a question of studying column/beam systems with regard to column distances and placement, shaping and dimensioning of steel sections, and principles for placing the bracing system. The higher the building, the more important and more dominant a factor will be the bracing system.

One of the advantages of a steel skeleton is that long beam spans can be combined with small column sections. Moreover, the low weight of the structure itself provides a more accessible loading capacity. By its openness, the structure also allows for simple, straightforward installations. When it comes to construction, a steel skeleton, or steel frame, is highly prefabricated and therefore, short on construction time, a feature that also positively affects the economics of the given building project. Another advantage is that steel can be produced with very small dimensional tolerances, guaranteeing a high precision building that, for example, will facilitate the fitting of the facade. The steel frame is also flexible in the sense that it can be changed according to its application. Such an adaptation prolongs the life of a steel building, and in the event of future razing, the steel structure can be easily dismantled and the steel reused.

The vertical load in a steel structure is transported through the columns down to the foundation. The most suitable structural layout for a steel frame is a square or rectangular orthogonal grid. The rectangular bay may often be the most economical solution because the decking then usually spans only in one direction. The columns are placed in the grid's points of intersection.

A bearing system often consists of continuous columns and beams spanning between the columns. The system has simple details and few elements. What is more, its assembly is easy and the column-to-column distance often fits the standard section lengths. In most instances the bearing elements are not pure steel structures. The floor slabs are generally done in concrete, either as precast floor slabs, such as Spancrete, or as precast concrete formwork that require additional in-situ concrete. The use of corrugated steel sheets as permanent formwork for a concrete deck is also common. In addition to the vertical load, the deck also bears the horizontal wind loads, and has the task of transferring them from the facades to the building's bracing system. The bracing system, in turn, transfers the loads downward. Frequently, a bracing system in steel is preferable to, for example, concrete slabs in stairwells. Steel angles are generally used as wind braces, either alone or joined, with screwed or welded connections. The steel weight per square meter / foot of floor area is an important economic factor in a bearing system. For example, the weight of the steel for a 4–6-story steel-frame office building is on the order of 20–25 kg/m^2 / 4.5–5.5 lb/sq. foot. Although the material costs make up only about one-third of the cost of the completed steel structure in a building, and the total bearing system only constitutes 6–10% of the total construction cost, it is good practice to strive for economical use of materials, and for simple, functional and, above all, production-friendly details.

The most common column sections are the W-shaped sections and several shapes of joined sections. In multi-storied buildings, the slenderness ratio of columns is not an important factor because we can expect lateral support from each floor deck. Thus, the steel stiffness is effective with slender column sections. In general, hollow sections have a lower steel weight than W-shapes, but the material cost is higher.

As beams, S (I-beam) are most common. The easiest approach is to lay the floor deck on top of the I-beams and to avoid underlying beams; this solution is best for dividing walls or outer walls that must hide the beams. W and M-shapes are also used, and C or MC-shapes are used where the floor deck comes only from one side. Inside, it may be advantageous to build the beams into the floor deck and weld. T-shapes are commonly used.

Chicago skyline with Sears Tower at far left and Standard Oil Headquarters at far right

*Standard Oil
Headquarters, Chicago
Architect: Edward
Durell Stone*

*Facing page:
Continental Building
Architect: C. F. Murphy
Associates*

The Chicago School

Chicago offers an outstanding case study of the history and development of modern architecture. Many consider it to be its birthplace, and a number of the first, largest and finest buildings that we find there validate that claim. Some of this century's greatest architects lived and worked there—Mies van der Rohe (1886–1968) Frank Lloyd Wright (1867–1959), and Louis Sullivan (1856–1924), Wright's teacher and one of the founders of The Chicago School.

The Great Fire of 1871, which destroyed the greater part of the city's center, brought about the plans and reconstruction projects that gave name to The Chicago School During the 1880s, a large number of 12-, 14-, 16- and up to 23-story buildings were erected. These buildings did not start as isolated examples; rather, they were related to one another on the basis of a common fundamental concept.

The new building type was the office high rise, based on new materials and a new technology. Bearing walls of massive brick were gradually abandoned in favor of frames of bolted steel sections. Fireproofing was accomplished by cladding the steel

The Fair Building,
Chicago, 1891
Architect: William Le
Baron Jenney

80

skeleton with brick or natural stone. The first high rise to be built based on the new thinking was a 10-story building, the Home Insurance Building of 1885, with William le Baron Jenney (1832–1907) as architect and engineer. The client asked for a fireproof office building with maximum daylight in each room. The building was designed as a free-standing steel-frame structure. However, the building authorities called for additional brick bearing walls for the lower four floors.

In the Second Leiter Building of 1891, with eight stories, Jenney carried out the first thoroughly steel-framed structure without using brick bearing walls. Thus, the groundwork was laid for the new building type with effective utilization of three-dimensional steel skeletons in combination with extensive use of glass in the outer walls. In time, the steel-frame found a consistent and characteristic expression on the facades with its rigorous and well-proportioned adaptation of the Chicago window. During the hectic period between 1883 and 1893, the architects and engineers of the Chicago School created a number of buildings of very high architectonic standard that had an enormous influence on the architecture of the twentieth century. Today some historians refer to this period as The First Chicago School.

Lake Shore Drive, Chicago, 1968 Architect: Mies van der Rohe

During the three decades following World War II, Chicago was once again the pivotal location for the development of tall buildings. Due, in particular, to the architectural firm of Skidmore, Owings & Merrill (SOM), ever-higher structures have been built in the areas surrounding the Illinois Institute of Technology (IIT). This period has been called The Second Chicago School, and steel was once again the preferred structural material.

In 1951, Mies van der Rohe established the concept for his tall structures at 860 Lake Shore Drive. In the two 26-story apartment towers with views of Lake Michigan, he expands and renews his ideas from The First Chicago School with the three-dimensional steel skeleton and entire facades of glass. While the steel columns are covered in concrete for fire reasons, steel is clearly articulated in the facades. Vertical S-sections on the facades give the towers a visual lift while, at the same time, helping to stiffen the frame, and facilitating the installation of the glass panels on the facade. Here the steel frame finds another expression on the facades by drawing the entire glass skin behind the surrounding S-sections.

As early as 1948, Myron Goldsmith, senior partner of SOM, and Jim Ferris made conceptual drawings for a tall structure in which the diagonal bracing designed to take the wind forces was exposed on the facades. As towers grow taller, the wind loads become so great that they cannot be ignored. The number of diagonals increased toward the ground, where the forces are greatest. In 1969, SOM and engineer Fazlur Khan put this concept into practice in the John Hancock Center, exposing the diagonal wind bracing on the facades to give the building its distinctive image. With its exposed bracing system and wide base, the building narrows gradually upward toward its 100-story height. John Hancock's geometrical shape and its 18-story-high diagonal braces give an image of absolute stability. The building's architectural and structural messages are happily united here.

Five years later another megatower was erected. With its characteristic stepping configuration, the Sears Tower, designed in 1974 by SOM and engineer Fazlur Khan, dominates Chicago's skyline. With 110 floors, this has long been the world's tallest building, impeccably clad in black anodized aluminum and bronze-colored glass. The structural principle, in line with the ideals of The Chicago School, is based on the steel skeleton utilized as bundles of tubes in which each tube or pipe, with a cross-section area of 26 x 26 cm / 10 x 10", functions as an independent tall structure. The tubes are tied together to form an effective stiffened structure of enormous dimensions. From the base, 9 tubes in a square grid rise 49 stories. From there, the building continues with 7 tubes in a Z-shape plan up to the 65th floor. From the 65th to the 90th floor, 5 tubes form a cross-shape plan, while the uppermost stretch of 20 stories consists of 2 tubes.

Facing page: John Hancock Center, Chicago, 1969 Architect: SOM Engineer: Fazlur Khan

Sears Tower, Chicago,
1974
Architect: SOM
Engineer: Fazlur Khan

84

Stranden, Oslo

On the wharf front in the center of Oslo stands a steel skeleton 10 stories high. The steel is clad in glass and brick, and is visible only occasionally when it surfaces from the brick as balcony railings or as a base that supports the brick surface. The spearlike stays emerging rhythmically through the facades are secured to the steel skeleton in order to carry the load of the large cantilever. Architect Kari Nissen Brodtkorb, working with the engineering firm of Arne Hill, successfully combined these two materials in Stranden to receive both the Norwegian Steel Construction Prize and the European Steel Prize.

Stranden, dating from 1990, stands serenely at the end of Aker Wharf on the waterfront. The building contains 1500 sq. m / 15,000 sq. ft of residential space and 5000 sq. m / 50,000 sq. ft of shops, restaurants, and offices. The site was previously dominated by a large shipyard. The architect succeeded in her intention to utilize and emphasize the special qualities of the site, using forms and materials that recall maritime structures, and that immediately relate to the old red brick workshop spaces that, in their rebuilt version, face the same wharf front. The building's structure consists of a beam and column system with a bay size measuring 5.2 x 5.2 m / 18 x 18'. The steel structure replaces an initial bearing system in concrete that, late in the design process, was terminated for economic and functional reasons. In addition, exterior details could more easily and naturally be connected to a steel skeleton than to a building in concrete. The steel columns are

Stranden, Oslo, 1990
Architect: Kari Nissen
Brodkorb, Inc.
Engineer: Arne Hill,
Inc.

tubular square-sections with a symmetrical 200 x 200 mm / 8 x 8" cross section. The beams are about 180 mm / 7" deep, with an asymmetrical cross-section. These are beams with a narrow upper flange and a wide lower flange, made up of welded plates. The wide lower flange forms a shelf to receive the floor deck, and has a thinner plate than the upper flange so that the cross-sectional area is just as large in principle, at the beam's upper and lower sides. The connections between beams and columns are bolted. As far as was possible, welding was used only on details that could be completed at the steel factory. The actual connecting plate between the column and the beams was inserted through a cut in the columns and welded to it. The floor decks are poured in place concrete and steel, so-called composite steel and concrete decks, which constitute the formwork for in-situ casting of the full thickness of the deck. The building's bracing is provided by strategically placed steel wind braces.

The steel in the interior is fireproofed with heavy mineral wool and plaster plates, and is not normally visible because the columns and beams are embedded in the walls. The steel details of the main bearing system are not given an architectural finish, but rather are left in a kind of raw state. Nevertheless, all visible surfaces and spaces are well composed and comprise an attractive whole that complements the distinctive qualities and character of the site. The architect herself says that the choice of materials was "picked up" from the site. "Hand-pounded brick and specially colored mortar are the block's enclosing overcoat. Polished white-painted surfaces act as a reflecting lining in the block's interior. Black lacquered steel and massive oiled woodwork on the balconies, elevators, and bridges offer contrast and warmth. The street, like the apartments, needs materials that are in a dialogue with the hand and skin. The closeness to the materials is essential."[13]

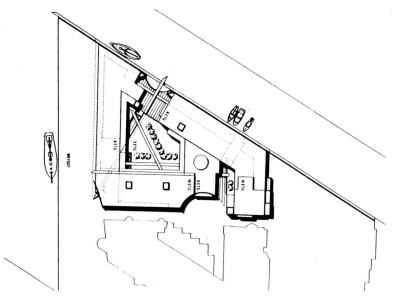

Stranden, Oslo, 1990
Site plan

86

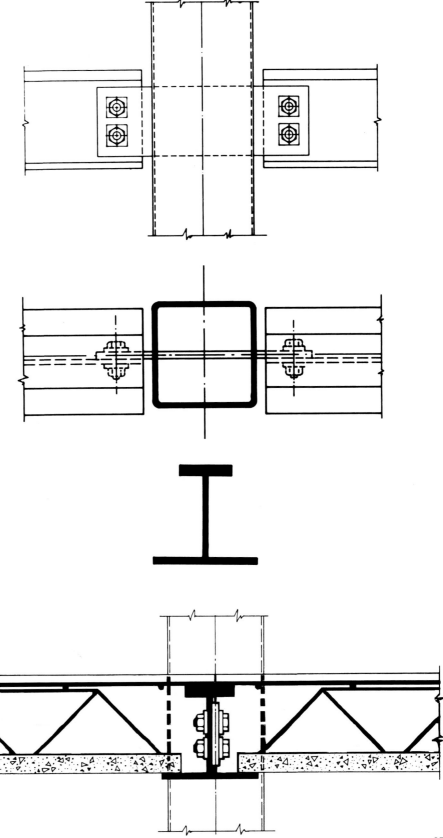

randen, Oslo, 1990
etails: Connection
tween beams and
lumns, beam cross
ction

tranden, Oslo, 1990
Detail section through
'eck at column
onnection.

SOM in London

Broadgate Development is a spread of office buildings and shops surrounding the Liverpool Street railway station in London. As a kind of backdrop to the open railway hall lies a remarkable building designed by the well-known Chicago-based architectural firm of Skidmore, Owings & Merrill (SOM). The building has 12 floors all of which are supported by exposed steel arches that span the entire length of the building. The reason for this rare structural choice is that the building had to be supported without columns over the track area leading out of the station, which run right under the building. The steel skeleton of columns and beams is also exposed on the exterior, and for fireproofing reasons is also drawn well outside the facade.

If we disregard the ordinary composition of the facade, we are confronted with an interesting structural concept: Four arches support the building—two exposed in each long facade and two "hidden" in the building's section. The uppermost part of the building, i.e., everything above the arch, is supported by columns which, in turn, are supported by the arch. The entire lower part of the building is suspended from the arch. Compression-loaded columns on the upper side thereby become tension-loaded members on the lower side, while their cross-section remains the same. This is possible thanks to the bracing action of the floor plates along the length of the columns, thereby preventing buckling. The bracing is also visible on the exterior in the form of diagonal compression struds. The detailing also betrays the various local conditions in the vertical bearing structure. Steel plates that make up the local bracing of compression loaded elements are relieved under the arch by precise, bolted connections that enable joining of the tension members.

The arches consist of two steel sections that are joined to one another to form rigid, spacious cross section. The arches are parabola-shaped and are connected at the base by a continuous tension member. The incredible slenderness of the arch is made possible by the small diagonal compression struds which prevent it from kicking outward along its entire curvature. The parabolic shape also makes the arch moment free when the load is evenly distributed and symmetrical. If the load is not symmetrical, the suspended diagonal bracing will effectively limit deformation of the arch.

Even if carrying out this structural concept presented additional problems of thermal breaks and fire protection, the Broadgate project stands as a fine example of the multifarious roles of structures. In addition to supporting the building, this form solves a functional problem, namely the necessity to create a self-supported office block spanning across 70-80 m / 240–270'. The choice of form clearly makes reference to the neighboring railroad station, as the arch form on the office building relates to the main hall of the station.

Broadgate Development, Exchange House, London Architect: SOM

Richard Rogers in Japan

Following Frank Lloyd Wright's Imperial Hotel (1915–1922) and Le Corbusier's Museum of Modern Art (1959) came a 20-year period lacking in important examples of Western architects' work in Japan. Western architects had to be satisfied with building works for Expo and for use as diplomatic missions for various countries. At the start of the 1980s this situation changed radically. Despite the fact that Japan has many architects of its own, the commissioning of highly qualified Western talent has become more common. Among those that built in Japan during the 1980s are Christopher Alexander, Mario Botta, Michael Graves, and Norman Foster.

In 1987, Richard Rogers rented an office from the K-One Corporation and established a practice in Tokyo. K-One, a real-estate development company, has seen the value of working with internationally known architects such as Zaha Hadid, and is responsible for the majority of Rogers' Japanese projects. Rogers says the company's leader, Soichi Hizaeda, is "one of the very rare types of developers who has a vision and makes architecture possible."[14]

The Iikura offices of the British car maker, Rover, are a good example of the cooperation between Rogers and the K-One Corporation. The building fills a cramped lot between the oval Noa Tower office block and blocks of a more ordinary character. In this location the Rogers Rover offices stand out with an articulated facade of glass and exposed steel structure "detailed with a jeweler's precision."[15] The facade is light and transparent in character. Rogers himself says that "our building is to a great extent a work of filigree; it expresses the structure and the joy of the movement up the elevators. We tried to create a relationship between the filigree work in our building and the massiveness of the neighboring buildings."[16] Keeping the structure on the exterior allows for a completely column-free floor area, which permits the efficient utilization of the L-shaped plan. In a similar way to Rogers' Lloyds building in London, the service areas to the stairs and elevators are placed outside the office areas, in separate satellite towers.

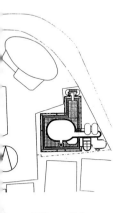

The steel construction is the building's most striking visual feature, and is probably the first to appear exposed in Tokyo without any special form of extra fireproofing. The structure supports the floor decks, which consist of grids of steel beams that direct the load down to the smaller columns. Between the columns, spanning beams

Iikura Offices, Tokyo, 1993 Facade

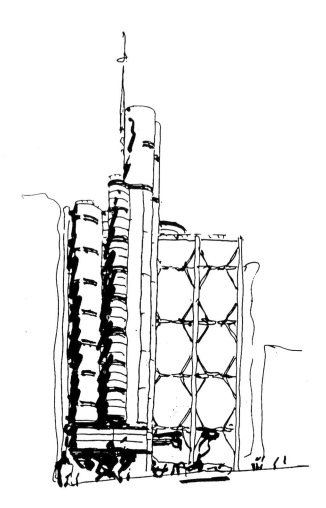

are joined to them by diagonal stays of tubular steel. All joints were welded on site. The form of the structure consists of frames that stiffen the building against wind and earthquakes. The natural flexibility of the steel skeleton makes it the ideal material for this kind of construction. The biggest problem with exposed steel structures, however, is meeting the fire codes. Here, the design team has really broken new ground. The structure has achieved a two hour fire rating, with the help of a "fireproof" steel and a 2 mm- / $3/32$"-layer of fire-retardant paint. It is the first building in Japan to use a new steel from Nippon Steel, which has used alloying and advanced Western steel production techniques to achieve excellent fire-retardant properties. The steel consists of about 1% by volume of alloying metals in the form of chromium, molybdenum, and nickel, 10 times that of normal construction steel. The result is a substantially more expensive steel, but a steel that retains its firmness to a greater degree when exposed to high temperatures. Fire-resistant steel is a relatively new material in architectural connections and there is reason to believe that increased use in the future will make its cost competitive with solutions based on fireproofed construction steel.

92

The engineers for the Rover building, the structural design department of the Toda Corporation, joined forces with Ove Arup & Partners and the Umezawa Design Office. The architect and the engineers designed a steel structure that, for aesthetic reasons, is as slender as possible. To accomplish this the thickness of the steel elements was increased, in some cases up to 40 mm / 1–1/2". The building's structure also addresses the prevailing special static conditions—with typhoon and earthquake loads. The structure enables a "free plan," a minimal solution with regard to dimensions—thanks, in part, to the absence of extra fireproofing—a solution that offers maximum access to light and a transparent facade, a structural solution that articulates the facade in a meaningful manner.

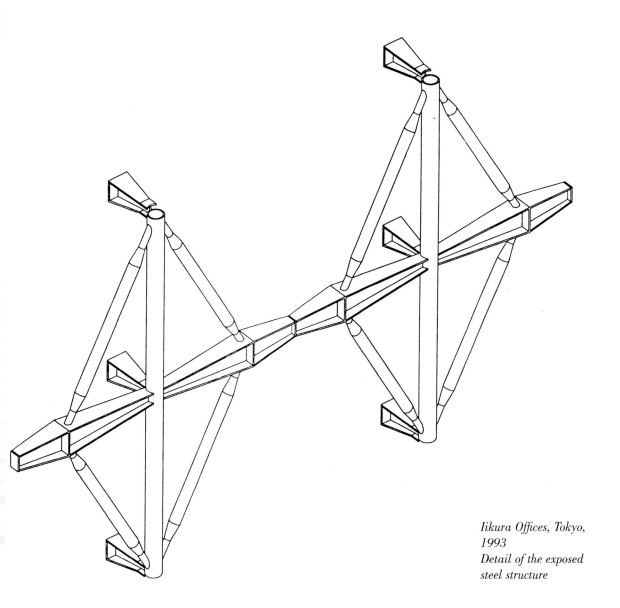

Iikura Offices, Tokyo, 1993
Detail of the exposed steel structure

La Grande Arche,
Paris, 1989
Architect: Johan Otto
von Spreckelsen
Engineer: Erik Reitzel
External elevator
tower. The slender
appearance of the
tubular construction
becomes further
reinforced by the shiny
stainless steel surface.

There are three important reasons for treating the surface of steel: fire protection, corrosion prevention, and to make it look good. For a description of the corrosion process, see page 35. What follows is a discussion of the various methods of treating steel surfaces.

Paint Treatment

The most common way to prevent steel from rusting is to paint it. Today's paints can have a long life if we choose and apply the paint according to the manufacturer's directions. This is financially important, with regard to both initial cost and future maintenance. Preliminary treatment, paint quality, coat thickness, and the paint job itself are all important determinants of the quality of the corrosion treatment that can be achieved.

To help determine the basic requirements of a preliminary treatment, five degrees of corrosion—related to the environment to which the steel will be exposed— should be considered.

Corrosion degree: 0
Indoors, with a relative humidity below 60%
Very little corrosion risk

Corrosion degree: 1
Indoors, unheated, with good ventilation
Little corrosion risk

Corrosion degree: 2
Indoors, with varying temperature and humidity
Medium corrosion risk

Corrosion degree: 3
Densely populated or industrial areas over water or near the coast
Great corrosion risk

Corrosion degree: 4
Exposed to constant humidity, near industries that produce or use chemicals
Very great corrosion risk

Powder Lacquering

A method of permanently surface treating steel and other metals is powder lacquering. Lacquer is applied to the material electrostatically as a dry powder and is subsequently hardened at 160–200° C / 295–366° F. The process is done at the factory, where it can be controlled with precision. In contrast to the more traditional surface treatments, with which it can be difficult to cover every bit of the surface, powder lacquering is evenly melted over the entire surface of the material. Powder lacquering not only provides very good corrosion protection, but also leaves the material with a shiny, even surface. The method requires no solvents.

Heat Galvanizing

Steel can be protected from rusting by coating it with another metal. A very common method of doing this is to dip steel into a bath of molten zinc, which is heated to approximately 450° C / 820° F. This process is known as heat galvanizing. A layer of pure zinc and iron alloy forms on the surface of the steel, adhering well and becoming completely watertight. Normally, the method provides a relatively thick coating (100–200 microns). However, the structure and composition of the steel will influence the thickness of the coating for a given dipping time, and these factors can therefore be used to control the thickness of the zinc. Alloying of iron and zinc forms a brittle and hard film, and shaping of a galvanized steel part can lead to the destruction of a relatively thick protective layer. For thin steel plates, therefore, a method is used that gives an alloy layer of only a couple of microns, so that the plates can be shaped after galvanizing without damaging the coating.

Heat galvanizing is an economical way of protecting building elements from corrosion, but it requires that the components be placed in the zinc bath without too much difficulty. Heat galvanizing is used mainly for light and medium-weight steel structures, i.e., for structural parts with no more than 20 sq. m / 200 sq. ft of surface area per ton of steel weight. A good example is trusses.

Heat galvanizing provides a cathodic protection that is self-repairing if scratched. Structures that are heat galvanized can be painted, but experienced builders will allow the parts to stand for about a year so that the zinc can "raise hairs," which provides good adherence for subsequent painting.

Cor-Ten

Copper and copper alloys oxidize in the atmosphere and form a stable patina tha when scraped, is self-renewing and thus provides "built-in" rust protectio Weathering steel, or Cor-Ten, withstands corrosion because it has a higher conte of copper and phosphorus than other types of steel. Cor-Ten can be easily identifie by its rusty red or purple color.

Cor-Ten has been used in industrial installations, but it was the Finnish-bo architect Eero Saarinen (1910–1961) who introduced Cor-Ten in buildings with h design for the headquarters of John Deere & Company. The idea when using Co Ten in buildings is to let it rust for a while so that it "sets." However, its use has n been problem-free. Building components that are exposed to precipitation ca acquire a different patina than those components that are protected from rain. It important, therefore, to use it properly and with careful consideration for detailin

John Deere and Company, Moline, Illinois, 1962 Architect: Eero Saarinen

Stainless Steel

Adding chromium to steel forms a strong film of chromium oxide on the surface that is rust preventive. Steel that contains more than 12% chromium is called stainless steel, and is generally used for special building parts that need to be maintenance-free, such as fittings, railings, mantles, etc. The use of stainless steel is expensive, and this usually limits its applications. However, compared to a finished surface-treated steel product, stainless steel can still prove cost-effective. Whether it is well or poorly processed, it shows its unmanageable nature and material tensions in streaks or uneven surfaces.

The O'Hare Rapid Transit Extension Station, built in 1985 by the architects Murphy/Jahn, connects one of the world's busiest airports with Chicago's Loop. An upper landing affords a good overview of the station, an underground revelation with undulating walls of glass block. The dominating material is stainless steel—benches of perforated plates, signs, railings, etc. Even the trains that pulse in and out of the station shine in their stainless cladding. The almost glowing lighting of the multi-colored glass bricks, the shiny steel, and the motion of the trains and people combine to create a mood of saturated intensity.

Louis Kahn's (1901–1974) Yale Art Center, dating from 1953, and the Yale Center for British Art, from 1974, were built across the street from one another on Chapel Street in New Haven. The older building is faced with red brick while the newer has an exposed concrete skeleton filled with panels of oak veneer on the inside and stainless steel on the outside. The steel has been given a gray matte finish approximating the color of the concrete and is in the same plane as the window glass. Kahn sought a color tone that would correspond to lead or pewter: "On a gray day it will look like a moth, on a sunny day like a butterfly."[17]

*O'Hare Rapid Transit
Extension Station,
Chicago, 1985
Architect:
Murphy/Jahn*

*Yale Center for British
Art, New Haven, 1974
Architect: Louis Kahn*

LONG-SPAN STRUCTURES

London Transport
Museum
02.03.84

Form, Structure, and Dimension

Steel is especially well-suited for building types requiring moderate to very large column-free space. It has the greatest strength per unit area of any material and a favorable relationship between strength and weight, making it possible to construct buildings with large spans not only economically, but also with a visually light, elegant appearance.

This chapter features buildings that demonstrate steel's potential for long spans, beginning with a brief overview of the purest structural systems for horizontal load-bearing.

Let us consider large halls, i.e., single-story buildings with large, free spans that are not braced by intermediate elements or interior walls. Therefore, it is the horizontal structure that is of greatest interest to us, especially when it comes to frames and connections between horizontal and vertical bearing elements. In this type of building the figure of the structural system complements the building's total form. Thus the relationship of structure to form is especially obvious in this type of architecture. This means that all structural choices take on a design significance, and vice versa, and that the design of details and individual elements takes on special importance.

The tables that follow show the natural range of use for various structural systems. In addition, rules of thumb are suggested for the relationship between structural height and related span. The suggested factors must be regarded as a kind of more lenient load that is evenly distributed. For more complex load situations and bigger loads, the stated factors may be deceptive. In any case, the rules of thumb are only for help in the early stages of the design process. Keep in mind that they can never replace statistical calculations.

In the first example we see the simplest system, using straight steel beams supported by walls or columns. The beams can be standard rolled sections or welded plate girders. The roof surface can be placed directly over the beams, which is climatically propitious and helps stiffen the compression-loaded upper flanges.

Comparison of two structural solutions for long spans in steel. 3D modeling: Stein Erik Sandaker

Top: Project for oil museum and boat terminal, Stavanger, 1992
Architect: Edvardsen, Hoglund, Witzoe
Engineer: B.N. Sandaker

Bottom: Project for oil museum and boat terminal, Stavanger, 1992
Architect: Arne Petter Eggen
Engineer: Kristoffer Apeland

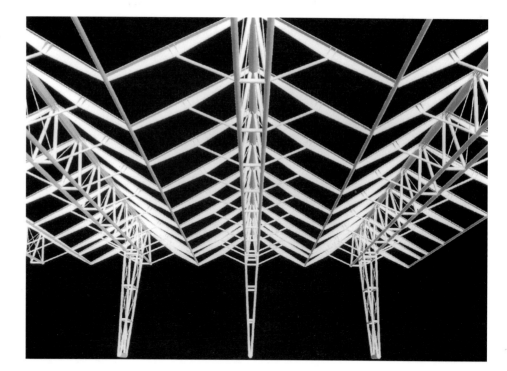

103

Basic types of structural systems. Range of span (L_0) and the relationship between member depth (h) and span length (L). The stated upper limit of the range of span (L_0) applies to roof structures. For floor structures, the upper limit is considerably lower.

	L_0 [M]	h/L
	3–50	1/20–1/30
	6–60	1/35–1/50
	8–75	1/10–1/15
	10–70	1/25–1/35
	10–90	1/15–1/20
	20–120	1/15–1/30

104

	L_0 [M]	h/L
	5–40	1/30–1/40
 t/a ≈ 1/15-1/30	8–55	1/10–1/20
 H/L ≈ 1/4-1/6	25–70	1/50–1/70
 H/L ≈ 1/4-1/6	40–120	1/30–1/50
 H/L ≈ 1/5-1/10	20–150	t/L 1/1000–1/10000
	20–150	t/L 1/1000–1/10000

In order to increase the span while keeping the dimension of the steel beam at a minimum, the beam can be supported at one or several places along the span, thereby forming a trussed beam. The posts set-in under the beam become compression members, united by a continuous tension member that is either a wire or a thin steel member. With such a structural approach, the beam must be dimensioned to withstand compression loads in addition to bending.

Greater load-bearing capacity and an increase in span can be achieved with the use of trussed structures. The truss can be planar or spatial, and is formed by staves joined in rigid triangles. Compared to pure beam construction, trussed structures are visually lighter and of greater bearing capacity, but require a deeper section.

If the architectural plan allows, additional supports can be located in a square or rectangular grid in which the difference between the sides is not greater than 1:1.5. In this case a two-way structure of beams might be suitable. For maximum rigidity it is advantageous to make the orthogonal joints moment-connections. If the beams have a cross-section that works well against torsion, as in rectangular sections, the two-way system will have great load-bearing capacity.

The same grid construction can be done with crossing trusses. If the trusses in this type of system are closely spaced, running in the same direction, and interconnected in the other direction with additional steel members, then we have a spatial system called a space frame. Space frames have a large two-way load-bearing capacity and are extremely lightweight.

Used in situations with individual column support, all these types of horizontal structural systems require separate bracing systems. In principle, this can be achieved in a steel building with cross-bracing. The bracing system must respond to compression and suction forces along the two main plan directions, and must be placed in such a way that the braced wall areas do not have a common point of intersection. In practice, this means that at least three different column areas must be braced.

When using frame construction, bracing for horizontal loads can be taken care of by the main structural system itself. Structural frames are designed for lateral bracing, which is achieved by the joint action between the horizontal and vertical members. If a corner can be made a moment connection, so that it will not change its angle under load, the structure will also be able to withstand lateral loads in its own plane. A structural frame can have a maximum of three connections that are not moment connections—in other words, it can only have three pin connections. Like with beams and columns, the frame can also be made of trusses.

The arched structure with three pin connections has the same capacity for lateral stability that a frame has. The arch will function structurally only when its endpoints are prevented from being displaced outward. The arch can consist of steel sections or be made up of individual steel staves. An arch carries its load when compression forces are generated in its cross-section to a greater or lesser degree, depending on how close the shape of the arch matches the compression curve of the load in question. Normally there will be bending moments in the arch in addition to compression forces.

Thus, frames and arches have the capacity of withstanding lateral forces acting on their own plane. To withstand lateral forces acting on the direction perpendicular to the structure's plane, several frames or arches in a series must be braced among themselves.

Arches and frames can be juxtaposed to form spatial structural systems such as cupolas or structural grids of frames. A suspended steel cable is a kind of reverse or up-side-down arch that can only withstand tension stresses. While the arch will tend to splay its endpoints, the endpoints for the cable will tend to be drawn in toward one another. This can be counteracted, for example, by using a combination of columns and backstays. The use of backstays can also provide lateral bracing in such cable structures.

A fundamental problem with the use of cable structures is the cable's pliancy, which causes the cable to change shape every time the load changes. To avoid this, the cable must be stiffened either by increasing the loads on the cable through pre-tensioning, or by constructing an inverted bowstring truss. The principle here is that the suspended main cable is connected to another cable of opposing curvature. This secondary cable is pre-tensioned and transfers the resultant force to the main cable putting it under tension. The system will then become rigid along its own plane. Cable trusses can also be grouped together to form multi-bay spatial structures.

Another method of bracing a cable roof is by using double-curved structures. One set of cables is suspended in one direction while another pre-tensioned set arches in the opposite direction and holds the main cables taut. In the following sections, several of these structural principles will be shown in their architectural contexts.

The Great Exhibition Halls

Crystal Palace, London

"The year 1851 marks a turning point in the history of modern architecture," writes Christian Norberg-Schulz.[18] There are several reasons why this is true and why it represents an accurate description of the significance of the Crystal Palace in subsequent architecture. For one thing, the building of this gigantic hall was a triumph for industrialized building construction, in which all building components were mass produced at the factory and assembled together at the building site. For its speed, organization, and the enormous number of components required, this accomplishment has hardly been surpassed even in our time, and presumably can only be compared to the construction process of off-shore oil rigs. The building's architect, Joseph Paxton (1810–1865), who had built noteworthy greenhouses in the service of the Duke of Devonshire, created an architectural work that manifested the dawning modernism's new openness and flexibility, and thereby anticipated the world view of the next century. Symbolically, this was expressed in the transparency of the big building—the simultaneous experience of inner and outer space, the feeling of infinity in a space created by man. Of this transparency Norberg-Schulz says that it bears "witness to the symbolic importance of the translucent material that so convincingly solidified existential space in the new world."[19]

Crystal Palace, London, 1851
Architect: Paxton and Jones
Engineer: Fox and Henderson
Interior view

The great international exhibition in London introduced an epoch characterized by more or less regular corresponding exhibitions, especially in France. It is as if the great architectural achievement of 1851 in Hyde Park inspired later curators and sponsors to pay special attention to the architecture in their exhibitions. The exhibitions that followed thus became important events that presented the new potential in industrialized building construction, both from the architectural and the structural point of view.

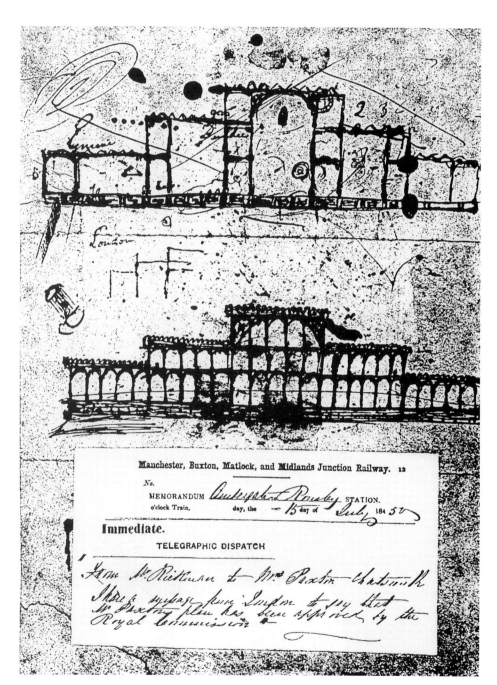

Crystal Palace, London, 1851 The "blotting paper sketch" that was Paxton's first conceptual sketch. Inset is the telegram to Mr. Paxton dated July 15, 1850, with the message that the project was approved that day.

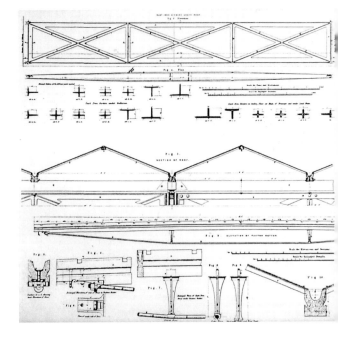

Crystal Palace,
London, 1851
Cast iron girder across
24'-span, and the
purlins, or "Paxton
gutters," of wood.

Crystal Palace,
London, 1851
Live load tests of
girders.

The significance of the Crystal Palace to the development of architecture is closely associated with the use of cast iron and wrought iron, which were later refined to what we know as modern construction steel. The rapid and precise production of building components calculated for rational assembly was only possible with the use of iron. Similarly, the expression of transparency, openness, and the minimized use of material was dependent on iron, which could offer slender structural elements with great strength.

110

The London exhibition in Hyde Park could never have been realized if Paxton had not suggested the use of a building material that was just as easy to disassemble as it was to assemble, and that also could be reused. By the spring of 1850, opposition to the exhibition had grown quite strong, not least because of arguments concerning the permanent character of the buildings had they been built in brick and stone, as proposed by the exhibition committee itself. The initiative for a large exhibition—to stimulate international trade—came from none other than Prince Albert, and a royal commission was established to plan the event. An architectural competition for the exhibition building was announced, and 245 entries were submitted. Unbelievably, all entries were rejected, and the building committee set up by the Royal commission did the project itself. On the building committee were prominent architects and engineers like Charles Barry (1795–1860) and Isambard Kingdom Brunel (1806–1859). The project, which consisted of an enormous, multi-naved brick building with a gigantic iron cupola, met with immediate resistance in the press and the public sector. Moreover, the limited time remaining precluded the realization of such a building.

This was the situation when Joseph Paxton launched his concepts with the aid of the so-called "blotting paper sketch," a pen-and-ink drawing covered with ink stains, which suggested the principles for a large exhibition hall. This was in June of 1850, and seven days later the most important sketches were made following the approval of the building committee.

The building, completed by New Year's Day in 1851, was 565 meters long and 137 meters wide. The length (1851 feet) symbolized the year of its construction. To take full advantage of standardization, it was decided to use an eight foot module, determined by the maximum spanning capability of a glass panel. The immense roof was composed of gable roofs of glazed lights, spanning between iron girders, and supported at eight foot intervals by wooden beams/gutters that are tensioned by trussing on the underside. This ingenious device came to be known as the "Paxton gutter," and was used as both an internal gutter for condensation and an external one for rain water. It functioned as an inverted roof truss as well. The tension on the underside of the wooden gutter created a shallow arch to help drain the water. The girders were 24 feet long, three eight-foot modules, done in cast iron, and given their maximum span. The girders over the middle nave were 72 feet long and therefore had to be made of wrought iron. Everything rested on hollow cast-iron columns of varying material thicknesses, but with the same outer cross dimensions, and the building was braced by light wrought-iron diagonals.

After the exhibition the building was dismantled as expected and reassembled at another site in a modified version. It was accessible to the public until 1936, when it was completely destroyed by fire.

La Galerie des Machines, Paris

The Crystal Palace represented an architectural breakthrough for the uncompromised building of iron and glass, and will be remembered for its incredibly short construction time, thanks to mass production, prefabrication, and mechanization. The Galerie des Machines, from the world's fair in Paris in 1889, represents the very essence of accumulated knowledge about structural principles and materials throughout the 19th century. With a free span of 115 m / 385' repeated over a length of 420 m / 1400', and with a height that reached to a maximum 46 m / 153', this building exceeded in size everything that had been previously built.

This seminal work in the development of modern architecture is first and foremost attributed to the engineer Victor Contamin (1840–1898). Having taught Strength of Materials at L'Ecole centrale des Arts et Manifacture in Paris, Contamin was appointed a member of the commission responsible for the control of strength calculations for the Eiffel Tower. He served with the corresponding professors at L'Ecole Polytechnique and L'Ecole des Ponts et Chausees. Concurrent with this task, Contamin was chosen by the director of Paris construction workers, Adolphe Alphand (1817–1891), "to study structural details of metal structures for three palaces at Marsmarken, to obtain estimates and supervise construction and assembly."[20] The architect Ferdinand Dutert (1845–1906) was appointed to assist him.

Galerie des Machines, Paris, 1889
Architect: Ferdinand Dutert
Engineer: Victor Contamin
Interior view

The groundwork began in July of 1887, and consisted of two rows of 20 foundation blocks, one for each of the 20 frames. The foundations were built to withstand vertical and horizontal loads of 412 tons and 115 tons, respectively. Contamin was adamant about wanting to take down the loads to a single point in order to facilitate the calculations, and in the process created one of the first three-hinged frame structures. This structural solution, which implies a narrowing of bearing structures downward toward the ground, departed so fundamentally from classical building principles that it gave rise to considerable contemporary concern and criticism. Actual assembly of the frames started in April 1888 and was completed in September of the same year. For budgetary reasons the Galerie des Machines was built of iron and not steel, which was still too expensive.

Galerie des Machines, Paris, 1889
Section of the three-hinge frame with a 115-meter / 385-foot span.

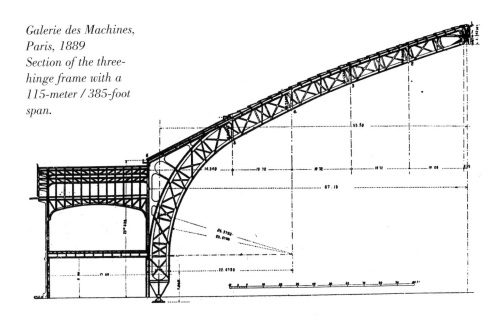

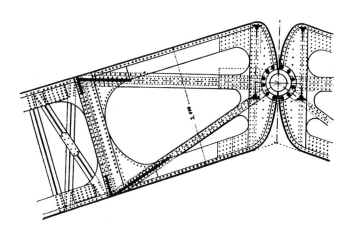

Galerie des Machines, Paris, 1889
Detail of hinge connection at the top of the frame.

Within this enormous space the public was freighted on large, movable platforms, "les ponts roulant," that made it possible to view the exhibited machines from above as you moved along the entire length of the hall. Kenneth Frampton says Contamin's hall "not only exhibited machines, the hall itself was an exhibited machine."[21] Entirely clad in glass, this building did not create a delineated interior space, but implied a blurring of the distinction between inside and outside. Siegfried Giedion says that "the esthetic significance of this hall lies in the union and amalgamation of the building and the outer space."[22] In the same manner, the 3.5 meter- / 12 foot-high cross-section of the frames swings upward in a supple arch, and makes the classical separation of what supports and what is supported meaningless. The frame "springs up toward its load only to unite with it," says Giedion.[23] The relative lightness of the structure allows the light pouring in from above to erase the structural elements, so that it looks as if the enormous frames were floating. P. Morton Shand comments: "The structure had once again received its expression, its own style. Contamin's Galeries des Machines was one of the most beautiful shapes in which mankind has ever enclosed space; but while space has hitherto been enclosed as if in a bird cage, here it floated as freely as the surrounding air."[24] The building was torn down in 1910.

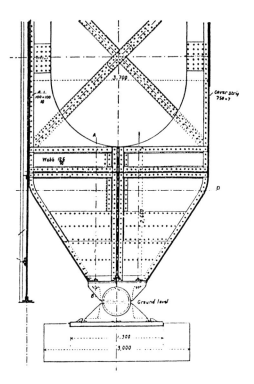

Galerie des Machines,
Paris, 1889
Detail of hinge
connection at the base
of the frame.

114

La Halle des abattoirs de la Mouche, Lyon

Three years after the machine hall was regrettably torn down (in what has been described as "artistic sadism"), Tony Garnier designed a steel hall with many of the same characteristics of the Galeries des Machines. The shape of the 210 meter- / 695 foot-long hall is formed by three-hinged truss frames with a span of 80 m / 265'. With its 17,000 sq. m / 170,000 sq. ft, the building has one of the world's biggest column-free floor areas. Garnier designed the hall as a part of his plans for an industrial city, and it was completed in 1914 for the opening of an international exhibition. However, World War I followed soon thereafter and the hall was converted to an ammunition and weapons factory. Not until 1927–28 was the hall put to its originally intended use as the slaughterhouse for Lyon. The slaughterhouse was closed down in 1974 and the building was declared a historic monument the following year to keep if from being torn down. It remained empty until 1987, when it was restored as a multifunctional recreation hall.

Garnier's hall had a much lower cross-section than the Galeries des Machines— only a little over 20 m / 66' high and 80 m / 265' span. Relatively speaking, this leads to greater lateral forces that must be transferred to the joints. Their detailing is done with the greatest possible clarity and stands out as structural meeting points with great intensity and ornamental value. Riveted together, the steel angles and T-sections provide an additional finished surface with a rich texture.

*La Halle des abattoirs de la Mouche, Lyon, 1914
Architect: Tony Garnier*

In contrast to the Galeries des Machines' use of glass over an appreciable part of the roof surface, Garnier let the light in through horizontal bands that follow the length of the hall. This is done by stepping the roof surface up from the gabled structure in such a way that the glazed bands read like risers in the large stepped roof-scape. This way the hall is well lit without having the uncomfortable intensity of direct sun light.

Tony Garnier's hall has been preserved as an ideal example of the great halls, spaces in which the structural solution and the architectural form are completely and intimately connected.

La Halle des abattoirs
de la Mouche, Lyon,
1914
Structural detail

Waterloo International Railway Station

The new tunnel under the English Channel makes it possible for Britons to reach large European cities by train in a relatively short period of time. To serve the new rail line British Rail has built a new international railway terminal for Waterloo Station in London, a 400 meter- / 1325 foot-long streamline-shaped, curved hall with a span that gradually changes from 55 m / 183' down to 35 m / 117' at its narrowest.

The railway terminal was designed by architect Nicholas Grimshaw & Partners, with engineers YRM/ Anthony Hunt Associates. In the best British/French tradition they started with a three-hinged trussed arch as a structural system. The structure is asymmetrical as it spans over the width of the hall, so that each arch has a small truss and a large truss. The top hinge in the arch, between the two trusses, does not fall as expected along the central axis of the structure, but is shifted toward one side. Both small and large trusses are built of tubular steel and are triangular in cross-section, but with a different composition of members that responds to two different load conditions. All the elements in the trusses are rectilinear, except for the largest pipes in the structure—the two top chords of the larger truss and the bottom chord of the smaller truss, which are curved.

The roof surface is mounted above the structure, over the large trusses. The surface consists of matted corrugated stainless steel panels between the trusses, and a band of overlapping glass panels right over the trusses. The roof surface over the small trusses is all glazed and mounted on the underside of the trusses. This side of the hall becomes a transparent facade facing west and toward the arrival.

Historically, we know that railway halls have often been important in the development of structures in architecture. The Waterloo terminal also represents such a developmental step. With its blue-painted structure, Grimshaw and Hunt have indicated a new optimism for high-tech in the public transit system and for railway architecture in particular. "The hall itself is a hymn to the marriage between architecture and engineering art, so well suited for transportation buildings."[25]

*Waterloo International
Railway Station,
London, 1993
Cross section*

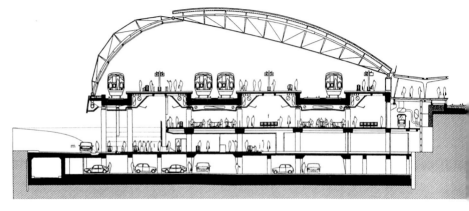

*Waterloo International
Railway Station,
London, 1993
Architect: Nicholas
Grimshaw
Engineer: Tony Hunt
Site plan*

The Convention Hall in Chicago

Chicago gave Mies van der Rohe (1886–1968) big commissions, and thereby the opportunity to put his European architectural ideas into practice. He designed the new campus for the Illinois Institute of Technology (IIT), 23 buildings laid out according to a planning module of 24 x 24'. The structural method chosen was steel skeletons with columns and beams at regular intervals, filled in by brick and glass. Among particularly interesting buildings is the Alumni Memorial Hall from 1946 with its famous corner details (the Mies Corner), and Crown Hall from 1956, the large, column-free space that contained the architecture and planning departments.

In 1953 the South Side Planning Board of Chicago asked Mies to do a conceptual sketch for a Convention Hall in an area between the IIT and the Loop. The metropolis needed facilities for the hundreds of exhibitions, conventions, and large political meetings taking place every year. One of the program requirements tells us something about the size of the task; on short notice it had to be equipped with 50,000 seats. The site was in an industrial and commercial area with many dilapidated residences. This was an ideal point of departure for Mies. Here he could develop his conceptual project on his own terms without having to glance too much at the surroundings.

In collaboration with his favorite engineer, Fred Kornacker, Mies worked out a monumental structure, bigger than any exhibition hall in the world at that time. The hall had a square roof structure with a two-way free span of about 250 x 250 m / 720 x 720'. The structural principle was the grid, with flat 30-foot high steel trusses, 25 in each direction and all alike. The space-frame was carried by 36 standing, triangular, planar trusses, six on each side. Each triangle stood on a stable concrete pylon at intervals of 120'.

During the design process, alternative studies were carried out of the individual building components, dimensioning of the trusses, evaluation studies of various facade materials, etc. The preferred material was dark gray marble with light streaks, studied in models with colored glass and aluminum. What remained firmly decided all along, however, was the idea for the large square structure that envelops the prevailing space.

The square plan with the hovering roof structure is a theme Mies had cultivated in several projects. An early project in which this theme was tested was the "50 Foot by 50 Foot House" from 1950, a free-standing residence with facades entirely of glass in which the roof structure, a two-way steel grid, covered the house's single unified space supported by four columns. Another one was the National Gallery in Berlin of 1969, in which eight free-standing cruciform steel columns support a two-way grid of welded girders. The square geometry is strengthened by the two-way direction of the roof structure. Here one axis direction is no more important than the other. Mies carried out this concept with merciless consistency through all building parts in these projects.

The model photo of the Convention Hall's interior gives us an opportunity to study the trusses a little closer. All steel sections, top and bottom chords, as well as the vertical and diagonal elements, are equal with a flange of 350 mm / 13¾". The diagonal members are laid at 45 degrees; this gives the simplest and most consistent joint for welding. The facade's marble panels are positioned on the center line of the steel member to achieve an equal visual effect from the inside and outside. At the roof surface, each 30' x 30' structural bay is subdivided by three parallel T-sections. To obtain the correct weld between the T-sections and the top chord of the main trusses, the top chords are turned so that their flanges have vertical position. Finally, we note that the direction of the T-sections in any given bay is rotated by 90 degrees in relation to the four neighboring bays. This assures an even loading of the top chords while maintaining neutrality in the direction of the two-way system.

The project was never realized, but has nevertheless remained a triumph of the union between architecture and construction, or in the words of Mies, "the structure is the building itself."

The steel consumption in truss constructions of this magnitude is enormous. With spans of more than 50 m / 167', the consumption of steel is so unrelatively high that it is quite reasonable to study other structural forms than trusses. The span in the Convention Hall was, as mentioned, 250 m / 720'. Students and teachers at IIT have since studied alternative structural forms for such large spans, among others with principles based on cables suspended from masts, but always in the spirit of Mies with the demand for a clear structure.

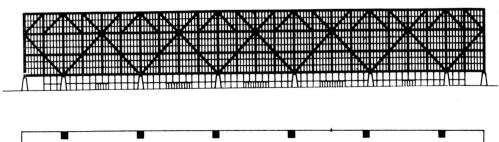

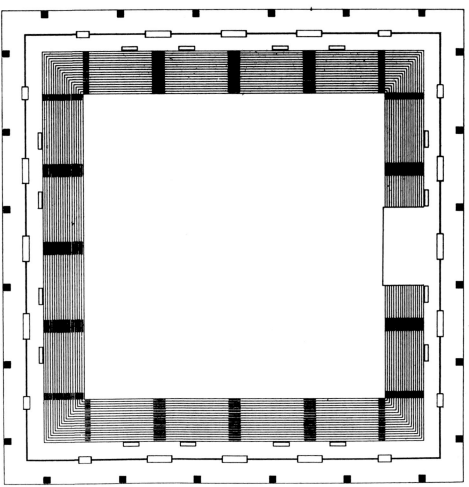

Convention Hall,
Project, Chicago, 1954
Architect: Mies van der
Rohe
Facade and plan

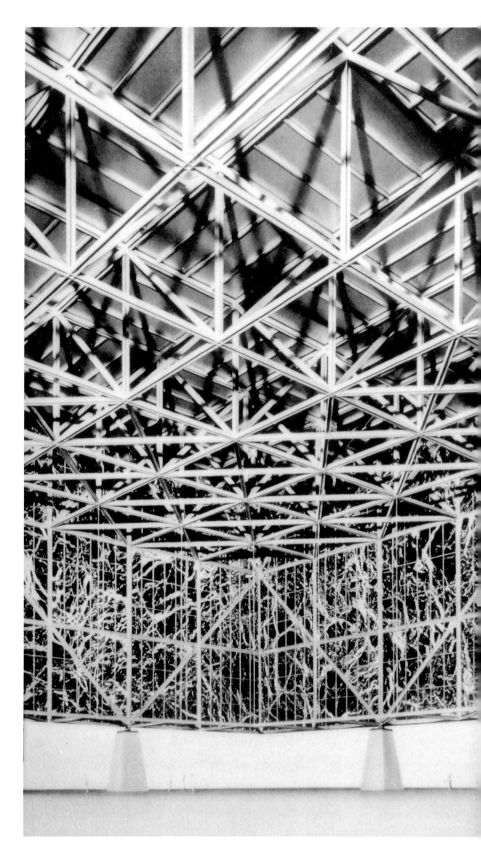

Convention Hall,
project, Chicago, 1954
Architect: Mies van der
Rohe
Model of interior

The Oslo Spektrum

With the Oslo Spektrum (1990), Oslo's eastern central area acquired a new hub of activity, bringing order to the dispersed spatial chaos that has heretofore characterized this section of the city. The Oslo Spektrum is an impressive work of monumental dimensions that displays fine architectural detailing from the largest scale to the smallest, from the gigantic steel structure to the hand-painted bricks on the facade. The new building is a "multiple-use hall characterized by optimal flexibility, with the geometry of a hockey rink as a point of departure."[26] The architecture firm, LPO, set out to design a hall that would accommodate sports events as well as concerts. This was possible because of the shape of the space, a sort of amphitheater with seating along the sides and toward the curved back wall, and also because of a very advanced grandstand system with a movable, flexible section.

A large steel structure rests over the entire complex. The trusses span about 74 m / 248' from the stage wall over to the steel columns spaced along the curved wall. The four longest trusses span over the mid-field of the hockey rink. These are double trusses, 6.2 m / 20' deep, with a box section to accommodate foot bridges, crain rails, and other technical and electronic stage equipment that is constantly being moved in this type of building. The steel structure is built of standard sections that are

Oslo Spektrum, Oslo, 1990
Architect: LPO
Architect Office, Inc.
Roof structure being assembled

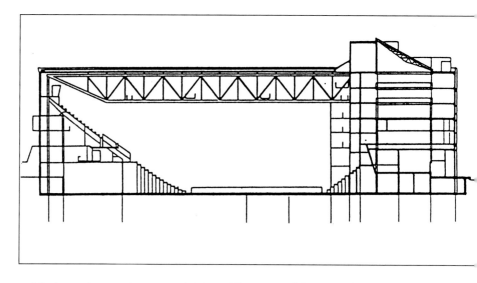

Oslo Spektrum, Oslo,
1990
Section

welded together at the trusses' joints. The top and bottom chords of the trusses are so large—330 x 500 mm / 13 x 20"—that they are plate girders. The trussses were produced and delivered in three parts that were bolted together at the building site. Across the main trusses and on their upper side, secondary trussed beams span about 13 m / 44'. They have a shallow gable shape to facilitate drainage off the steel plate roof surface. The enormous steel trusses, the largest of which weigh about 100 tons, carry the loads of all the technical equipment, including fixed and movable systems, in addition to the roof. The girders are dimensioned to meet the strict bending requirements for operating a transverse crane. In other words, the proportions and dimensions of the structure are determined not only by statics but also by the functional requirements of the hall.

The shape of the structure follows the geometry of the building's cross section, so that the underside of the trusses slope strongly to meet the columns, providing head-room for the grandstand and ensuring the spectators' line of sight. At the other end, the trusses almost collide with the stage wall, and the structure's underside is perfectly horizontal, which helps in the installation and operation of technical equipment.

The use of steel in the roof structure for the Oslo Spektrum is distinctly functional at all levels. All the design decisions are justifiable on the basis of building function and operation, as well as structural requirements. The structure takes on an exceedingly functional character in its own right, not as deliberate architectural expression. And this is how it presumably has to be with structures of this order of magnitude and with such a complex purpose. Perhaps for that very reason, it makes a strong visual impression that thrives in the atmosphere created by the robust and functional hall.

Oslo Spektrum, Oslo,
1990
Assembly of the 6-
meter / 20-foot-high
trusses

The British Pavilion, Seville

The 1992 World's Fair in Seville, Expo-92, celebrated the 500th anniversary of Columbus' discovery of America. The fair was arranged on the island of La Cartuja in the Guadalquivir river, the site from where, in 1492, the explorer set sail for the new world. The official theme for Expo-92 was "discovery," and in the British pavilion designed by architect Nicholas Grimshaw, discovery consists of showing that it is completely possible to unite a "high-tech" vocabulary of glass, textiles, and white-painted steel-pipe structures with today's ecological concerns for global resource and energy consumption. The steel structure is like a gigantic Erector set that can be disassembled as easily as it is assembled, an important property of steel structures that goes back to Paxton's Crystal Palace.

In the same way, the architectural expression of high-tech functionalism rests to a large degree on the esthetics provided by the passive energy systems. "This is typical of Grimshaw's design philosophy," says Colin Davies, "which makes no separation between technology and architecture."[27]

The entrance facade facing east consists of a continuous glass wall with a thin film of running water. This cooling system not only contributes to keeping the temperature down in the warm climate of southern Spain, but also provides an acceptable microclimate outdoors for the visitors waiting to get in. The water is collected in a tank and is pumped up to the top of the facade with electricity produced by solar cell panels on the roof. The roof is also shaded from direct sunlight by undulating sun screens. Facing west, the building has walls with large heat capacity, a well-known principle in warm areas where brick and stone have traditionally been used to delay heat transfer to building interiors. In this high-tech building the masonry blocks take the form of stacked steel containers filled with water. The water stores the heat until the outside temperature sinks, becoming lower than the inside temperature. Then the heat transfer reverses outward. With the sun shading of the south facade and the help of spread textiles, these passive systems serve to reduce the indoor temperature by 10° C / 18° F from the outdoor ambient temperature. The architecture of the British Pavilion addresses ecological issues in a serious manner by using modern technology and production methods, and thereby gives a double meaning to Grimshaw's intentions of expressing the "Spirit of the Age" in his architecture.

British Pavilion,
Seville, 1992
Architect: Nicholas
Grimshaw and
Partners
Engineer: Ove Arup
and Partners
Detail of the entrance
facade

The British pavilion is a box-shaped structure 65 m / 217' long, 38 m / 127' wide and 25 m / 83' high, and is built in a "high-tech" tradition in which all building components are articulated to express the technology that produced them. Nothing is made for the sake of effect; nothing is faked or hidden. What you see is what you get. Therefore the structure's architectural expression becomes just as important as the expression of the passive energy systems.

The main organization of the building is based on the principle of free-standing boxes in the large general space that constitutes the pavilion's total volume. The smaller volumes contain spaces for exhibitions and for video presentations, and are served by a system of escalators and ramps. The disposition of the large volume is done so clearly that the visitor never loses contact with the surrounding envelope, or with its precise, elegant steel structure. Spaced at 7.2 m / 24' on center, lightweight trusses with a curved bottom chord span the width of the building. The trusses have a W-pattern instead of an N-pattern, allowing for simpler welds and a lighter visual character. The trusses span outward beyond their supports to form an overhang that shades the long facades. The vertical supports of the structure can be described as walls made out of steel tubing that provides lateral bracing to the building at the abutment. Lengthwise the pavilion is braced with diagonal steel cables.

The joints between the trusses and their supports are moment connections at both ends. An advantage of this approach is that the wind loads can be distributed between both opposing supports. A disadvantage, however, is that the expansion of steel under high temperatures cannot be absorbed, and the structure must be dimensioned to take additional loads.

The actual building process was affected by the fact that that the steel structure was produced in England and then shipped to Spain. Each truss was made in two parts that were bolted together on site, reflecting the British preference to do the welding in the factory and the bolting at the building site. Consequently, all connections carried out at the building site were bolted or pinned to gusset plates.

The choice of structural system and materials for the British pavilion afford an esthetic reminiscent of shipbuilding, and especially of sailing vessels. From the undulating sun screens on the roof, to the lightweight steel structures, and the use of fabrics like sails on the short facades, plus the fact that the entire building "rests" on a reflecting pool of water, this pavilion is a reference to the technology and language of shipbuilding, and an affirmation of Great Britain's image as a maritime nation. Even the high end-walls are designed to be inherently stable

*British Pavilion,
Seville, 1992
Plan at the level of the
exhibition and video
spaces*

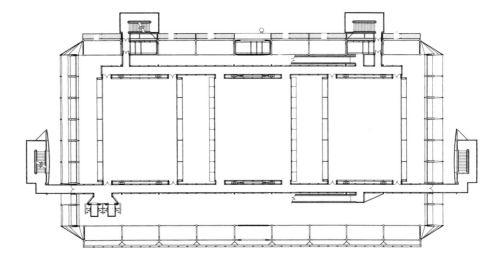

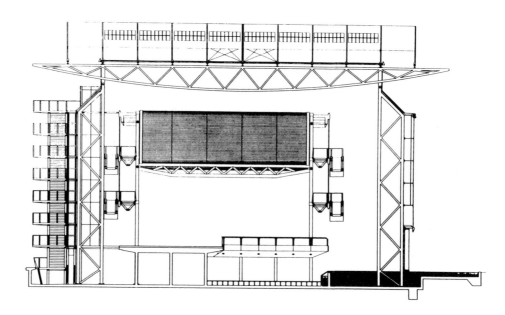

Tension masts are made of curved tubular steel that, aided by outriggers, are partly stiffened by external curved cables, and partly by tension straps that extend from the foundation to the roof and keep the form from straightening itself out.

The British pavilion at Expo-92 showed the visual power of tectonics in the "high-tech" tradition. More generally, though, it was a reminder of the infinite expressive potential of structures in architecture. It was torn down after Expo-92 closed its doors in October 1992.

British Pavilion,
Seville, 1992
Detail of steel structure

British Pavilion,
Seville, 1992
Exterior detail

Iglebaek at Ensjo, Oslo

Ensjo is one of those typical areas one finds on the outskirts of Norwegian cities with a mixture of industry, warehouses, and residences. In Ensjo much of the industry relates to automobiles. In 1991, Iglebaek, a Mazda automobile dealership, opened its new offices on Ensjo street. Built on a slightly sloping site, the new building includes a showroom, workshop, and offices.

The showroom, in white-painted steel and glass, is the building's natural eye-catcher. It is entered under a simple canopy that extends the full length of the north facade and is made of arched steel ribs supported by two parallel I-beams on double tubular columns. The showroom's very orderly and clear roof structure is based on a two-way system of welded steel trussed girders supported by columns on a 12 x 16-meter / 40 x 54-foot module. The columns and girders are made of tubular steel with a circular cross section. Lateral bracing is accomplished by triangulating stiffeners between the trusses' bottom chords and the column capitals, and by the rigid connection between the columns and the prefabricated concrete deck. All the exposed lighting installations and ventilation ducts have found a logical and well-ordered placement between the trusses.

*Igleboek at Ensjo,
Oslo, 1991
Architect: Torstein
Ramberg*

Igleboek at Ensjo,
Oslo, 1991
Section and plan

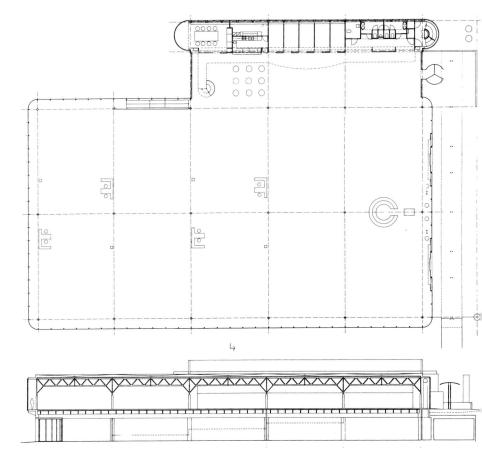

Igleboek at Ensjo,
Oslo, 1991
Sales hall and canteen

The facades, with their rounded corners, are supported by steel brackets cantilevering 1.6 m / 5'4" out from the concrete deck. This provides room for a circulation zone along the facades, from where one can see the cars without being inside the showroom. From this zone one can also closely study the construction of the glass facades. Free-standing pipes 82 mm / 3¼" in cross section, spaced at 2 m / 6'6" on center support the almost 5-meter- / 16-foot-high insulated glass panels. Sun shading is accomplished with the aid of external shutters.

The showroom's floor is finished in Italian ceramic tiles with narrow grout joints. In selected circular areas the tiles are highly polished and look like "reflecting pools." These areas are used for special exhibits. With its transparent character and consistently executed detailing, this is a beautiful space which the architect has controlled well. In retrospect one could perhaps wish that the client had been a bit more restrained in advertising the company name on the facade. In 1992 the building's architect, Torstein Ramberg (born 1941), was awarded Norway's National Building Style Prize.

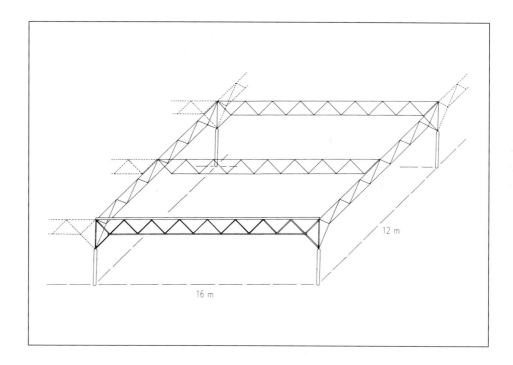

gleboek at Ensjo,
Oslo, 1991
The roof structure in
the sales hall is based
on a system of trusses
supported by tubular
steel columns with
triangular stiffeners.

12 m

16 m

Theme   *Steel as Sculpture*

The use of steel as a material for making art belongs to this century, when the tools of the steel industry became the tools of the artist. Today it is common for an artist to work with welding torches and masks, alone or in a modern steelworks. With it the machine culture brought exciting innovations which would affect not only how art is made, but also how it is perceived. In this new age it is possible for us to find beauty in a rusted plate of iron; to recognize poetry in the motley sounds of the mechanical workshop. However, a visible difference between the steel sculpture presented here and steel architecture is the artist's use of the steel *plate* versus the architect's use of the steel *section*. The reason behind each choice may boil down to a difference of opinion on the nature of steel—steel as *surface* contra steel as *line*.

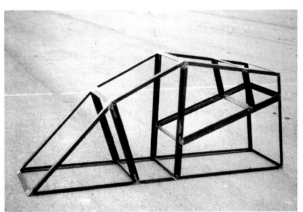 

Steel sculpture in sections, *1989–90, by Anne Marie Vadum.*

Alexander Calder

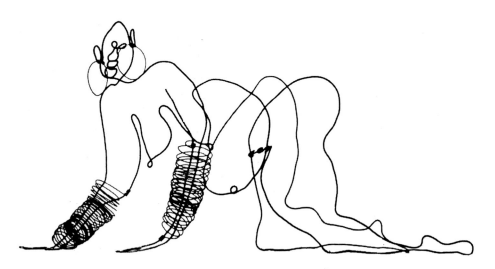

Alexander Calder (1889–1976), the creator of the famed mobiles and stabiles, is one of our greatest modern sculptors. His career began in the 1920s and 1930s with his miniature circus—a complete circus with strong men and slender ladies, wild animals and Indian elephants, all of it shaped like a kind of spatial drawing in steel wires. At that time artists were interested in the circus as a form of folk art and Calder, through his "circus performances," came in contact with other artists in Paris—Mondrian, Miro, Cocteau, Leger, and Duchamp. In this milieu Calder found inspiration for his subsequent work, the development of mobiles.

Calder entered an artistic collaboration with the wind, or better, the quiet draft in an indoor room, that contributed to the perceptibility of his works. The mobiles were finely balanced sculptures of rods, strings, and plates, painted in clear primary colors—red, yellow, blue, black, and white—that moved at the merest whisper of wind. With the mobiles, Calder succeeded in expressing a driving force within the figurative language of the 20th century: movement in time as in a fourth dimension. Calder himself described the mobiles as "four-dimensional drawings." What was sensational was not only that they moved, but that they commanded space without

Mobile
Alexander Calder

possessing great weight or volume. The mobiles are an expression of Calder's sense of humor, playfulness, and practical inventiveness. The fact that his background includes a few years' study of building statics early in the 1920s is not coincidental. The mobiles are in balance.

Another series of Calder's sculptures are the so-called stabiles, very much the opposite of the mobiles. They are static, cut out of iron plates that remind one of crabs, starfish, and other sea life.

Calder's sculptures, which are often of impressive dimensions, are on display in museums and public spaces on both sides of the Atlantic. In metropolises like New York and Chicago they appear at their best in the shadows of the sharply defined modern architecture.

Anthony Caro

After a sojourn in America, Anthony Caro (born 1924) returned to London in 1960 and purchased welding equipment and a load of scrap metal. He then made his first sculpture, *Twenty-Four Hours,* and in subsequent years continued to work in the material with which he is now so closely associated—steel. Sir Anthony Caro, "The Knight of Steel," designs and shapes industrial products into what is called "industry" sculpture. Every architect or engineer is familiar with the steel elements Caro utilizes in his work; they order theirs from the same steel supplier. His way of connecting I-beams, pipes, plates, and angled sections also seems familiar, be it by bolting or welding. This is hardly coincidental. Before Caro studied art at the Royal Academy he had taken the engineer exam at Cambridge. As a result of this versatility, Caro is capable of "crossing the language of the sculptural and engineering art."[29]

In his early years as an artist Caro worked as an assistant to Henry Moore. Around 1960, when his interest in steel became serious, he broke with the tradition that Moore represented, a tradition in which sculpture was created by modeling or carving. Steel and steel components suggest a third method for sculptural work, namely, by assembling, mounting, or structuring as in a collage. An important catalyst that led to Caro's turning point was the work of American sculptor David Smith, whom Caro had met during his time in the United States. Smith introduced Caro to the idea of welded elements as one of the possibilities in the sculptural collage technique.

In addition, to further understand Caro's art one must also examine the work of the cubists. There is no doubt that Smith and others who worked with sculptural collage had a great influence on Caro, but pictorial art, especially that of Cézanne, Matisse, and Picasso, also greatly influenced Caro's conception of space and artistic viewpoint. Cubism focused to a great extent on still life, essentially opening this genre to sculpture. An important name here is that of Henri Laurens (1885–1954), who in *The Guitar,* from 1914, utilized steel in a cubic sculpture that calls to mind Caro's first work in steel, *Twenty-Four Hours,* which came almost 50 years later.

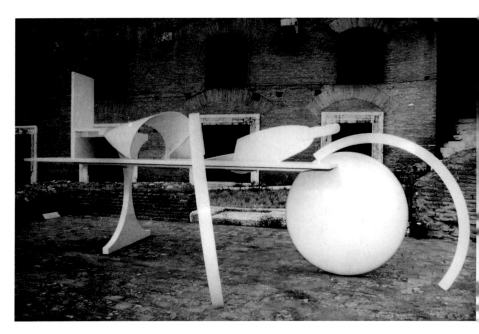

Sun Feast, *1969–70*
Anthony Caro
From an exhibition in
Trajans Market, Rome,
1992

Besides the collage technique, we see in Caro's work references to cubism in the gliding, floating layer or plan (the plan can only be discerned with the help of the line in a steel section, which partly overlap each other and thus mark the depth of the sculptural space), as well as in the prominent character of apparent weightlessness seen in several sculptures. In a way, this effect deprives the individual components of their mass and weight and thereby their physical significance, and we are forced to experience the composition as a single spatial unit. Caro's sculptures "lack" pedestals or plinths completely, and rest directly on the floor or ground. The impression of weightlessness is achieved because the supporting elements often are of the same dimension and character as the elements that are only shaped for the composition. Thus it is difficult to point them out; the sculptures seem to lack under support. The classic idea of supporting and supported elements is broken, the hierarchy is abandoned, and all steel components acquire the same physical significance. A further reinforcement of the equality, of the feeling of missing material presence, is achieved by the steel being painted—especially the 1960s sculptures—with strong, homogeneous colors.

On the other hand, there are essential differences between Caro's art and the legacy left by cubism. While cubism abstracted and reinterpreted nature, i.e., from our everyday materialism, Caro's works are completely liberated from a likeness to known objects. His sculpture is a constructed form that exists only in its own right, not as something that represents other objects. The sculptures should then be seen as alluding to the relationships between their individual components. Tim Hilton says that Caro's sculpture, therefore, has "no relationship to the world of utility in which the majority of objects and structures exist."[30]

138

Deep North, *1969–70*
Anthony Caro

Still, Caro's relationship to steel as a material is an intimate one. He has often expressed how he needs to feel the metal, and that he usually needs a long time to acquaint himself with the steel parts that eventually are assembled into sculptures. A new phase was introduced in 1970, when he began to use steel's more unworked qualities. He let surfaces rust and added varnish, and the sculptures acquired greater thickness and mass.

Sun Feast and *Deep North*, both dated 1969-70, belong to the painted period. In *Sun Feast*, Caro for the first time used a tank bottom that belonged to David Smith's steel storehouse, which Caro took over after Smith's death in 1965. The sculpture is painted a brilliant yellow and stands out as a perfect combination of movement and stillness. *Deep North* consists of a fixed figure composed of a cantilevered horizontal plane supported by two vertical elements—one standing upright, seemingly shaped like a propeller blade, and the other extending from it, coiling away and ending in a spiral several meters beyond on the ground.

In 1972, Caro worked for a 14-day period at a steelworks in Veduggio, Italy. During this hectic period he created 14 sculptures. Among the best is *Veduggio Sun*, which is made of milled steel plates with rough edges. These edges, which characterize the Veduggio series, appear when the steel is extruded from the rollers in a glowing, plastic state. As a rule, they are cut away from the plate and remelted.

Veduggio Sun,
1972–1973
Anthony Caro

From 1973 to 1974 Caro worked in steel from the steelworks in Durham, England. In *Durham Purse* he gives a different perspective of the material. Thin plates are folded in pliable, wavy motions and laid on top of one another. The effect recalls thick, supple leather, reminding us of steel's unbelievable plastic properties.

Caro's relationship with architecture is an interesting one. Even though he created sculptures during the 1980s that "enclose space," one cannot say that his sculptures are architectonic in a building sense. Instead, the relationship to architecture comes through his use of standard steel components. Terry Fenton says of *Deep North* that "its structure plays with the scale of architecture. It utilizes the absolute relationship between the parts and the human body to create a unified and total effect."[31] It has also been said that Caro's "industry" sculpture contributed to esthetically strengthening high-tech architecture. That Caro occupies such a significant place in art is due not only to his opening new avenues for sculpture, but also to the fact that his art in many ways seeks diffuse boundaries between industrial production, architecture, and engineering art. "Art thrives on the discrepancies between its territory and the real world, and it exploits the tensions between these frontiers."[32]

Durham Purse,
1973–74
Anthony Caro

Richard Serra

"Steel is the material I am familiar with and have known a long time, with all its properties, its weight, mass, thickness, and strength," says sculptor Richard Serra (born 1939). Serra's breakthrough came in New York in the late 1960s, and he has since been a central figure in American and European art.

In the early 1970s Serra abandoned his studio and set to work on his monumental outdoor sculptures in raw steel plates, in the countryside or in urban settings. The sculptures assumed such large proportions that it became necessary for Serra to involve himself in the production process. The procedure of the work itself took on great importance. Serra followed production at the steelworks, involving himself in the lifting and transporting, cooperating with engineers and crane operators in order to raise his elements into a standing composition. Artists have always had to master the handicraft side of their of their profession, to know the expressive possibilities of the material, whether it be marble or bronze. For Serra it became necessary to utilize industrial work methods and manpower.

Serra's sculptures adapt to their environment; when it comes to a piece by Richard Serra, there are no neutral places. Every site has its unique character, distinctive from all others. The works are site specific and therefore cannot be moved to other sites without losing their meaning. Serra says: "I am interested in the experience of sculpture in the place where it resides."

Facing page: Shaft, *1989*
Richard Serra
The sketch was a gift from Serra to engineer Finn Rasmussen in connection with the installation of the sculpture on Bank Place in Oslo in 1989.

Not always easily accessible, Serra's sculptures often arouse public debate and controversy. They break from the commonly held notion that they must represent something and harmonize with or decorate their surroundings. The pieces are clean and simplified, curved and straight steel plates in combination. The elements come directly from the steelworks without any form of special treatment or finish. It is steel in its original, purest nature. Serra's ability to "grasp" the site and the situation is impressive. As an artist he strives to increase one's consciousness of the site itself in relation to the sculpture.

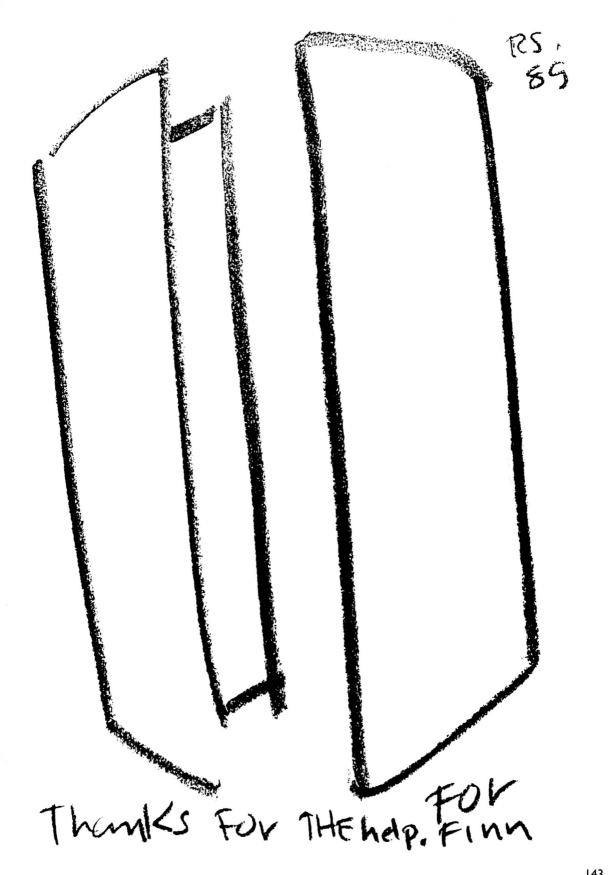

RS.
85

Thanks For THE help. FoR Finn

143

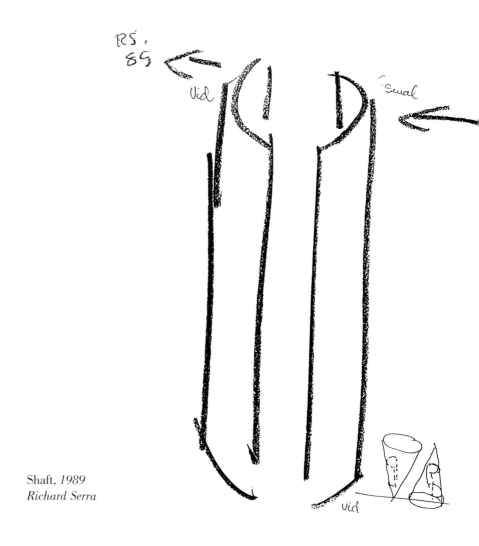

Shaft, *1989*
Richard Serra

The monumental sculptures are found in urban spaces in New York, Par
Barcelona, and Oslo. *Shaft* was installed in Oslo's Bank Place by the Museum
Contemporary Art in 1989. Between the sculpture's two curved shells one is able
glimpse the museum entrance. The 50 millimeter- / 2 inch-thick Cor-Ten ste
plates were milled at the Krupp Steelworks in Germany. What at first glance loo
like two cylindrical shells is really based on a much more refined geometry. Ser
cut the surfaces of two cones, turning one downward and the other upward. T
sculpture leans slightly toward the museum, yet still remains stable. Each sha
rests on three steel blocks. The calculations were made by engineer Fi
Rasmussen from Multiconsult, who also helped Serra maneuver the 14-t
elements into place. In its skewed position and its golden-rust Cor-Ten steel, *Sh*
is appropriately placed in Bank Place's otherwise commonly designed and rath
stone-dominated milieu, serving as an unavoidable signal of the museum's locatio

144

Artists 3 + 1

Gudbrandsdalen, one of Norway's principal valleys, has acquired another attraction. The Norwegian Road Museum at Hunderfossen, designed by architects Frydenlund and Hermanrud and opened in 1992, is well worth a stop along the E6 highway.

A group of sculptors were commissioned to adorn a section of the facade facing the valley. This group, which calls itself "3 + 1," consists of Paul Brandt (born 1941), Terje Roalkvam (born 1948), and Dag Skedsmo (born 1951), and has had a series of projects, generally on a common theme. A guest artist is invited to join in each project, this time Marus van der Made (born 1940) from Holland.

These artists take a constructivist approach to their task. The actual space is their point of departure. Together and individually they have had many commissions for adorning buildings in collaboration with architects. One of their best qualities is that they "understand what the architect is doing." They are involved in the material's properties and synthesis, and they often utilize series studies with frequent and repeated use of ideas.

Facing page: Artistic embellishment on the Norwegian Road Museum.
Left to right: Dag Skedsmo, Terje Roalkvam, Marcus van der Made, and Paul Brandt.

The facade of the Road Museum, which is made up of untreated concrete cast against upright forms, is divided into four diagonal niches with a window on the side. These niches comprise the point of departure for the ornamentation. The group chose stainless steel as the common material because it contrasts well with the untreated concrete and provides rich possibilities for reflection and play as daylight angles constantly shift. It is also readily visible from a distance. Each artist submitted a proposal for inside the selected 5 x 2.5 m / 16'6" x 8'3" upright forms. After discussing each approach and developing them further, they were incorporated into the final form and placed identically on each side of the wall surface. The abstract character of the reliefs mingles with the shape of the building and contrasts with the museum objects found outside. The ornamentation, created in collaboration with the architects, helps shape the museum's visual identity.

146

Wohlen High School,
Argau, Switzerland,
1988. Santiago
Calatrava

RIBBED STRUCTURES

atlas TGV Rhone-
lpes connection to
atolas, Lyon Airport,
994
rchitect and engineer:
antiago Calatrava

The Terminals

Several countries are now in the course of improving their public transportation networks. Even railroads seem to be experiencing a renaissance. The building of high-speed railways is being coordinated across national boundaries, and new stations and terminals are being planned and restored. Several exciting projects have been built along the new TGV line between London and Paris, among them a new international terminal at Waterloo Station in London (see page 117), and a new station installation in Lille's old center. In addition, many have followed Santiago Calatrava's "link" between TGV Rhones-Alpes and the Satolas Airport outside Lyon with a great deal of interest. But on the whole it is the larger cities that are paying the most attention to public transportation. In recent years they have become increasingly aware of the public environment. It hasn't been enough for public facilities to simply function; strong emphasis must also be placed on design and quality. Today, esthetic design is on the agenda, and it is no surprise that many of today's architectural and structural innovations are found in the area of public transportation. Stations and terminals are the exciting spaces that mark the transition from one form of transportation to another. These are the spaces that have given us truly great structures. We need only think of St. Pancras from 1876 in London, or the Gare St. Lazare from 1877 in Paris, immortalized by Claude Monet's paintings. To a large extent these are the cathedrals of iron and steel construction, then as now. Their halls are formed with ribs and frames, trusses and arches, often created in a strictly generated order, an order that perhaps finds its inspiration in the infinity of the tracks and the inexorable rhythm of the rail ties.

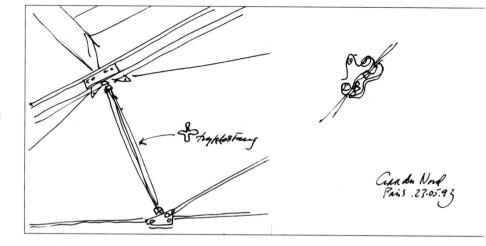

Polonceau roof truss in Gare du Nord, Paris Characterized by clear structural connections and play between tension and compression components.

Stadelhofen

Santiago Calatrava, born in Valencia, Spain in 1951, is an outstanding architect and engineer. In his projects he unites influences from such disparate sources as Antoni Gaudi and Robert Maillart. A dog skeleton in his office in Ilgenstyrasse in Zurich bears witness to an interest in organic forms. The Stadelhofen station from 1990, which is linked to the local railway network in Zurich, is one of Calatrava's most important works. The mere act of passing through the station and lifting one's gaze to behold its form is rich indeed.

*Stadelhofen Station, Zurich, 1990
Architect: Santiago Calatrava
View from the platforms*

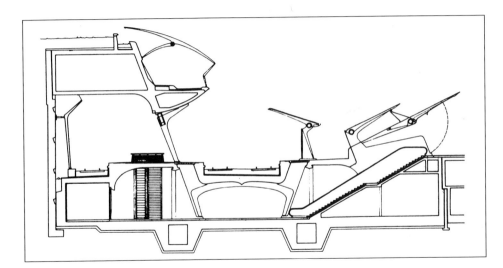

The station, with its 270-meter- / 900-foot-long platforms, is situated to take advantage of the terrain that slopes down toward the Limmat River in this part of Zurich. It is a project in which the solution lies "in the section" by using the differences in levels. The upper plan is a promenade with a pergola cover that echoes the park above. On the ground plan below is the actual station with three tracks on a level with the city streets. Below the track area there is a shop-lined street where the proprietors complain that they see more architectural students than customers.

The shape of the canopies and pergolas demonstrates a thematic utilization of organic structural forms expressed in steel. A freestanding steel and glass canopy over the platform on the city side consists of open web steel ribs cantilevered from a continuous pipe that follows the curve of the tracks. The pipe is carried by double columns 12 m / 40' apart; they are sculpturally shaped, diagonal pylons that lean toward vertical spears. Note that while the form of the steel elements is freely and organically expressed, the glass covering, which should be watertight, is purposely laid in one plane. The innermost two-sided platform is covered by a concrete deck shaped like a stretched-out tray. The tray is supported by powerful steel pylons with struts in three directions. In the same way that the rails are sloped, the steel pylons are placed at an angle. The solution of having the steel support the concrete above is reminiscent of Viollet-le-Duc's project for an open market hall with space above, described in greater detail in the chapter in this book on steel in combination with other materials. The steel pergola on the upper level is an impressive balancing act. The reason it doesn't tip over onto the tracks below is because there is a rigid connection, held fast by a ring of bolts, between the ribs and the pipe that supports them. The structure can thus be considered a three hinge arch. Today this may seem like an elegant but rather complicated arrangement to stretch a few wires for creeping plants. But in a few years, when everything is overgrown with flaming red ivy, the situation will be quite different.

The entire facility is built of specially adapted steel components. Here there are n standard steel sections. We may well ask how this can be managed, how it can be paid for. The transition from sketches to custom-cut elements can be executed by computer controlled cutting table on which up to four parallel blow torche following a digitized drawing, can cut identical sections from a steel plate. Ther are also digitally controlled saws and drills. A characteristic of these tools is tha they work with two coordinates in a two-dimensional plan, unlike digitall controlled robots used in the auto industry that work with three coordinates in three dimensional space.

Stadelhofen Station
Architect: Santiago
Calatrava
Pergola on upper level

Satolas

One of Calatrava's more recent projects which is currently under construction is the station for the high-speed railway, TGV Rhone-Alpes, and its link to Satolas Airport outside Lyon, France. The station's main hall is a 500-meter- / 1,666-foot-long vault of crisscrossing concrete arches, built at ground level above the underground platforms. Two huge wings surge upward from a triangular opening at the midpoint of the vault. This is the station's steel-ribbed roof that marks the transition from train to plane, from concrete to steel structures. From here the passengers are directed to a bridge over the access roads and parking to the existing air terminal.

*Satolas
Architect: Santiago
Calatrava
Passage between air
and train terminals*

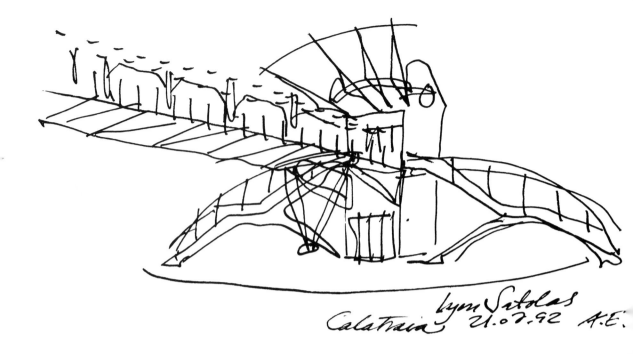

Calatrava Lyon Satolas 21.07.92 A.E.

Satolas, Santiago
Calatrava
*Stairwell and elevator
tower to pedestrian
bridge*

In the bridge's steel-ribbed roof we are reminded of Calatrava's design for Stadelhofen. But here the ribs' support is a high trussed girder, or open web joist that simultaneously supports the bridge itself. At the midpoint of the bridge, a passage to the stair and elevator core which leads to the parking levels below introduces a new structural variation. At this point, the steel roof is supported by a Vierendeel truss with triangulated corners.

Both the Spaniards and the Swiss lay claim to Calatrava, but based on this project it is perhaps more appropriate to place him in the French tradition characterized by Auguste Perret and Tony Garnier, as an architect-builder who seeks new architectural expression through the structural potential of steel and concrete.

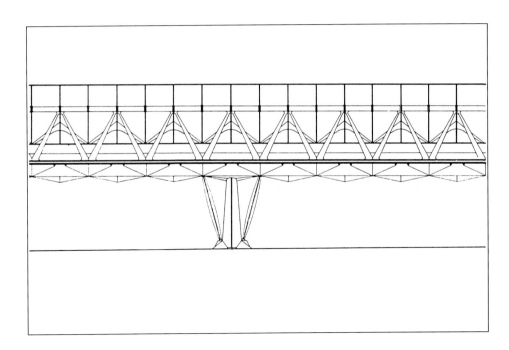

Satolas, Santiago
Calatrava
Pedestrian bridge

Satolas, Santiago
Calatrava
Stairwell and elevator
tower to pedestrian
bridge

157

Sloterdijk

Like the annual rings in a tree trunk, Amsterdam's great canal system—latter-day
avenues—lie in circles, one outside the other. The outermost ring is the most
recent, the Nederlandse Spoorwegens de Ringbaan. At Sloterdijk Station, dating
from 1987 and designed by architect H.C.H. Reijnders (born 1954), de Ringbaan
crosses two other lines. The terminal's three platform levels, with many associated
functions, are gathered within a large cubic volume formed like a table with four
legs. It is made up of a large steel structure that constitutes a prominent landmark
on the Dutch landscape. Ringbaan's two-sided platform lies on the uppermost level.
To shield passengers from the wind here at 12 m / 40' above the ground, the
platform and tracks are covered by glass. The platform is covered by a flat roof

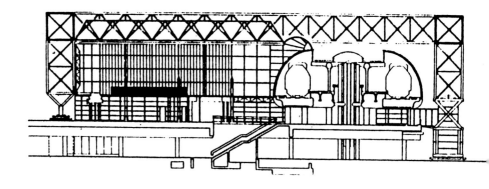

Sloterdijk, Amsterdam,
1987
Cross section

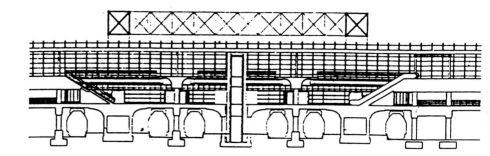

Sloterdijk, Amsterdam,
1987
Architect: H.C.
Reinders
Longitudinal section

supported by steel frames with cantilevered ends. The tracks are shielded by arch-shaped steel ribs that lean against the platform's roof system. The ribs consist of castellated I-beams with laminated glass mounted in frames on the underside of the ribs. The result is a beautiful 150-meter- /500-foot-long open space that follows the slight curve of the tracks, characterized by generous amounts of natural light and the rhythm of the steel ribs.

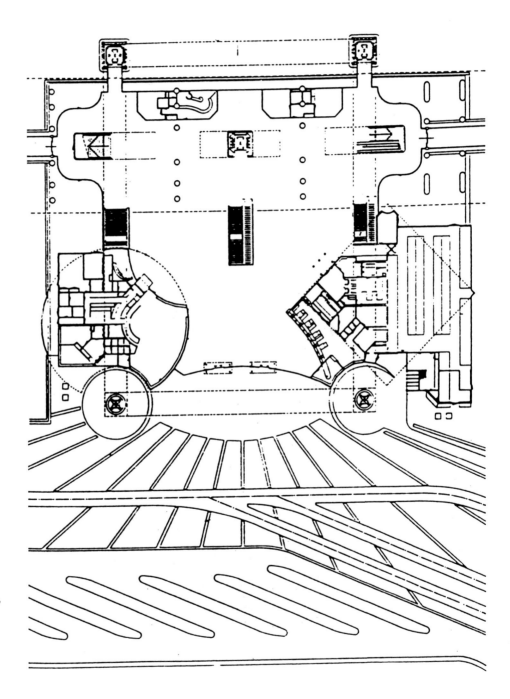

...loterdijk, Amsterdam,
...987
...rchitect: H.C.
...einders
...round floor plan

Sloterdijk, Amsterdam,
1987
Architect: H.C.
Reinders
Upper platform

Sortinget and Gronland

Oslo Sporveier (the Oslo Streetcar Company) is currently renovating its city's subway network, originally built in the 1960s and 1970s. At the Styorting and Gronland stations, dating from 1987 and 1992, respectively, and designed by architects Eggen and Mjoset and engineer Bonde & Company, the renovation of the platforms is being carried out in accordance with the existing design. The actual platform space is covered, which gives it a much more intimate character as a counterpoint to the station. When the train stops, the platform space is completely enclosed. Built like a mountain facility with halls and passages lined with concrete,

Stortinget Subway Station, Oslo, 1987 Architect: Eggen & Mjoset, Inc. Engineer: Ing. Bonde & Co., Inc. Interior

Stortinget's one-sided platform occupies a tunnel that is elliptical in section. The platform's space has ribs in sections that support a corrugated steel, vaulted ceiling which curves toward the back wall and the platform edge. The ribs also serve to suspend the signage, lighting, and other systems. The portions of the back wall that correspond to the steel ribs are done in enameled steel panels. The rib structure is the dominant element, the very architectonic backbone of the installation.

Gronland station, which is excavated from ground level, is a regular column/beam construction in cast concrete, with two tracks in the middle and platforms on each side. As at the Stortinget station, the corrugated steel, vaulted ceiling is supported by steel ribs, but here they are double ribs with a different shape. There is a horizontal console between each rib pair with room for lighting fixtures and for hanging signs and a clock. The steel ribs are connected to the existing concrete pilasters with a steel plate. The consoles have three different lengths that conform to the platform's varying depth. The outermost part of the steel rib pairs is bolted to

Gronland Subway Station, Oslo, 1992 Architect: Eggen & Mjoset, Inc. Engineer: Ing. Bonde & Co., Inc.

162

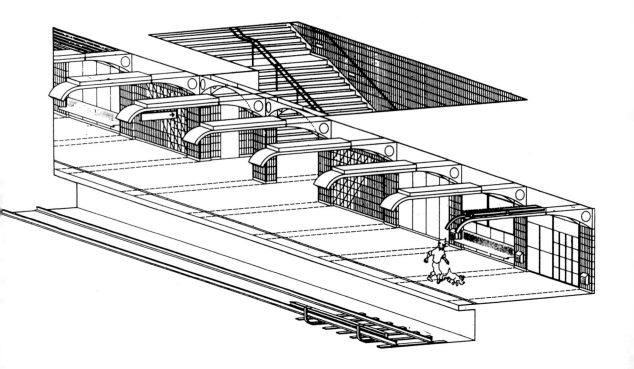

Gronlands Subway Station, Oslo, 1992 Architect: Eggen & Mjoset, Inc. Engineer: Ing. Bonde & Co., Inc.

the consoles' cantilevered arms which, at the front edge of the platform, are suspended from the concrete vaulted ceiling.

The installation demonstrates several different uses of steel. Ribs and consoles are done in lemon-yellow-painted steel-plate, wall elements of white-painted steel-plate panels mounted in painted steel-angle frames. Benches and litter baskets are of perforated, brushed stainless steel.

All of the architects we consider pioneers in the development of their art share one common trait: universality. Their driving force was the dream of shaping mankind's environment, from the great visionary city plans, via the individual buildings, down to the smallest objects of utility. In this century the chair has in many ways signaled the development of groundbreaking ideas. In 1929, Mies van der Rohe's Barcelona chair in chromed flat bar steel was one of the objects that introduced us to modern architecture. The steel-pipe chair was an important element in the period of modern architecture, on a par with the introduction of the free plan and the glass curtain wall.

Mies van der Rohe (1886–1969) sitting on his original steel tube chair from 1926. The photo is taken in his apartment in Chicago. "A chair is a very difficult object," says Mies. "A skyscraper is almost easier. That is why Chippendale is famous."

164

Barcelona Chair

The Barcelona Pavilion was Germany's and architect Mies van der Rohe's contribution to the world's fair in Barcelona in 1929. Placed on a terrace of travertine marble, the pavilion consists of a horizontal roof surface supported by eight free-standing, cruciform steel columns. The space is defined by non-bearing, leading walls of glass and marble. Here, Mies had carefully placed a number of his Barcelona chairs that were especially designed for the pavilion. The structural

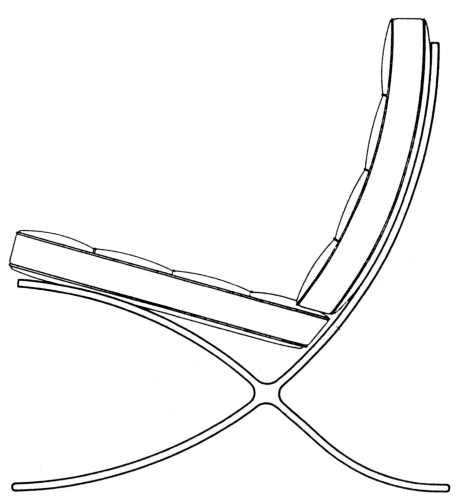

Barcelona chair, 1929
Mies van der Rohe

Lake Shore Drive, Chicago, 1953–56
Architect: Mies van der Rohe
The lobby is furnished with Barcelona chairs and a glass table from 1929.

concept consists of one pair of modified cruciform pieces of shiny, chromed flat bar steel, mutually united by three orthogonal flat bars at the top, middle, and front of the chair. A number of broad leather straps support the back and seat, which are padded cushions of natural-colored pigskin. The curvature of the chromed cruciform pieces, the elegant cushion work, and the beautiful proportions have made the chair one of this century's timeless classics.

Wassily Chair

Marcel Breuer (1902–1981), who got a pilot's license to be able to drive a car, has the honor of being the first architect to engage in the production of quality furniture that also was esthetically satisfying. As a student, and later as head of the furniture division at the Bauhaus school in Weimar in the 1920s, he acquired his basic knowledge of materials and their properties. "The load on a chair is greater than on the roof of an industrial building," he once said. Breuer, who at that time used to cycle to school, suddenly saw that the steel pipe of his handlebars could also be used in furniture design. In 1925 he presented his Wassily chair, named for the Russian painter Wassily Kandinsky, who also had an association with the Bauhaus. This was the first steel-pipe chair not intended for use in the kitchen or the dentist's waiting room, but rather for the living room. The Wassily chair combines light, springy strength with taut leather straps in the back, seat, and armrests. It is complex in form and construction, but beautiful in its subtle elegance.

Wassily chair, 1925
Marcel Breuer
(1902–81)

Propeller Stool

Several significant furniture artists hail from Denmark. Next to Arne Jacobsen and Hans J. Wegner, Poul Kjaerholm's (1929–1980) is the name that immediately comes to mind. He had an early international breakthrough, and his furniture is represented in galleries and museums the world over. His work is in the permanent collection of the Museum of Modern Art in New York.

Reclining chair PK 24
Poul Kjaerholm

His point of departure and moorings lie in the Danish furniture tradition, but they also encompass the international functionalism associated with Bauhaus design values. His furniture was developed with precision and consistency. He had perfect answers to all problems, whether they were technical, related to materials, or purely esthetic. His individual pieces were created with an eye for being part of an overall solution. He felt that elements had to exist in relation to one another.

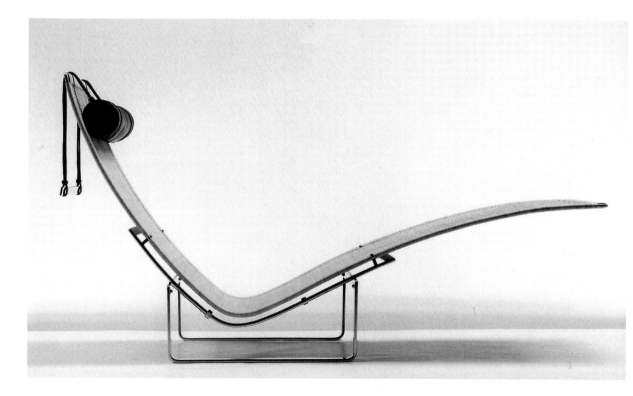

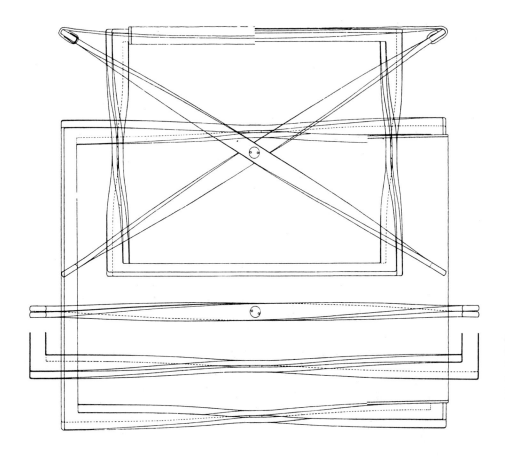

Together with a quality-conscious producer, Kjaerholm created pieces of furniture that would become classics, such as the easy chair from 1961 in matte-chromed spring steel with a back and seat of flag string. Here, legs, armrests, and the side frames of the back rest appear to be cut out of the same piece of steel plate.

Also from 1961 is his collapsible *Propeller Stool,* in twisted, brushed stainless steel with inlaid ball and socket joints in the point of rotation and a canvas seat. By utilizing a new technology, the stool became light and graceful, while the steel made it sufficiently heavy and stable to sit on.

The Well-Tempered Chair

The furniture of Ron Arad (born 1951) lies in the exciting boundary between design and art. His work is more about ideas, form, and the utilization of materials than about meeting functional needs. Arad is among the handful of artists who work on design projects all over the world. In his cellar store, One Off, near Covent Garden in London, you can see his furniture exhibited on a floor covered with sand.

The Well-Tempered Chair was commissioned by the German furniture manufacturer, Vitra. The chair will hardly find a place in most homes, nor was this the intention. A single stainless steel sheet is folded and screwed together to form an easy chair, complete with back, seat, and armrests. Aside from its obvious sculptural qualities, the chair is surprisingly comfortable to sit in; its amount of spring is just right. The chair is available in two versions—highly polished and matte.

The Well-Tempered chair
Ron Arad
Model by Svein Aage Johansen

MULTI-BAY STRUCTURES

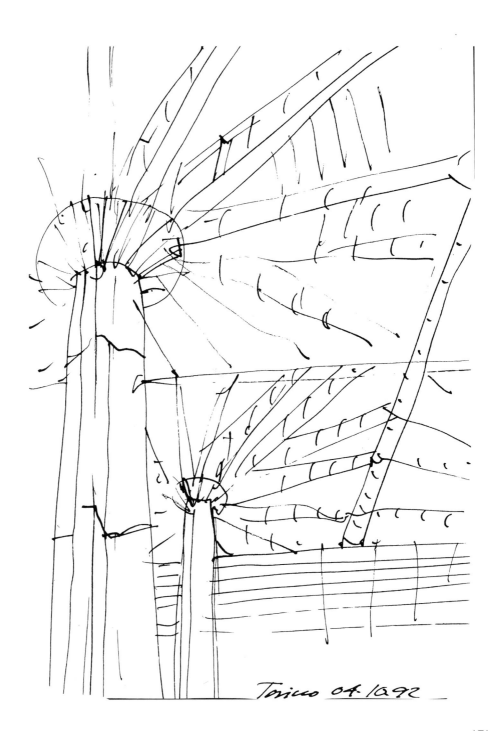

Palazzo del Lavoro,
Torino, 1961
*Engineer: Pier Luigi
Nervi*

"A Tale of Two Terminals"

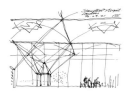

*Stansted Airport
Architect: Foster
Associates
Engineer: Ove Arup &
Partners*

Stansted Airport, London's third main air terminal, and Stuttgart's new airport, which opened within four weeks of each other in 1991, have several features in common. The design of both is based on a rectilinear, comprehensible connection between the check-in and departure areas. Their structural form is simple, appearing almost as a part of the landscape, yet as easily visible from the air as from the ground. But the most interesting feature in common is the use of structural trees that support the roof of the main hall. Many architects have found the latter feature engaging, and so here we take a closer look at how two of the most capable of them have interpreted that support system.

From Liverpool Street Station, one of the big railroad terminals of the 19th century, the Stansted Shuttle brings us out to architect Norman Foster's (born 1935) Stansted Airport, in the lush landscape of Essex. From the track one can get a brief glimpse of the terminal before the train glides into the underground station. Via ramps, bridges, and elevators, passengers are led up into the light of the terminal—which manifests itself as a huge connected space.

*Stansted Airport
Architect: Foster
Associates
Engineer: Ove Arup &
Partners*

172

Through the terminal's floor grows a forest of steel trees that supports a light, transparent roof. Each steel tree, which consists of four columns with four slender branches, supports the intersections of a quadratic horizontal grid of steel pipes with an 18-meter / 60-foot module. The tops of the steel-tree branches are braced by tension rods with a bolted connection. All the structural parts are made of white-painted tubular steel. With their four branches, the trees constitute the terminal's principal structure, while a secondary system forms a simple tensile structure that secures the branches in position and takes care of lateral loads. The Jesus bolt is the designer's term for this single bolt that holds the secondary structure together. If it should fail, it would assume the entire blame when the tree falls. By balancing strength and stiffness one arrives at a refined and simplified expression.

Vital to the realization of the clear and miraculously light structure is the fact that the roof carries no mechanical equipment. The ventilation plant is under the terminal's concourse level deck. All distribution equipment for heating, ventilation, air conditioning, and lighting serving the concourse level is contained within the steel trees. Overhead lighting assures an even daylight effect throughout the entire hall. At night, the lighting is reversed with the help of powerful uplights at the tree trunks. The light roof elements reflect the light down into the hall.

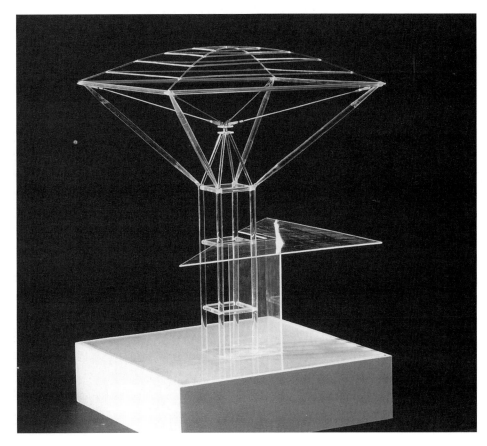

Stansted Airport
Architect: Foster
Associates
Engineer: Ove Arup &
Partners
Model by Synnove
Gjelland, Karoline
Ramsta, and Juli
Yrana

Stansted is in several ways characteristic of Foster's architecture as we know it from another of his well-known works, the Renault Center at Swindon, a large continuous space based on the addition of similar three-dimensional units. Each three-dimensional unit constitutes a typical structural form—masts with tension rods that are repeated throughout the entire project. This approach requires a significant effort for the development of individual units, but since they are all alike, the effort benefits the entire building.

Architects von Gerkan and Marg can hardly be called beginners, as Stuttgart is their seventh air terminal. The terminal building is shaped like a wedge in section, with a slanted roof reminiscent of an airplane's take-off. A series of semicircular terraces bend into the terminal, housing restaurants, shops, and other amenities necessary to all airports. However, the most important element is the tree-like structural system that supports the roof. The actual roof surface is divided into 12 equal rectangular sections measuring 26.6 x 43.4 m / 89 x 145', erected as a two-

Stuttgart Airport
Architect: Von Gerkan
& Marg

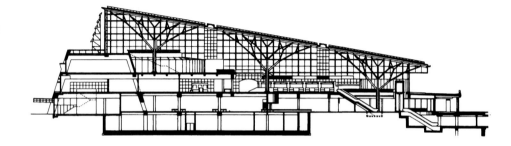

way steel section system. Each area is supported by a "steel tree," outlined by strips of glass, with the loads passing down through the branches to be collected in the tree trunk. The architect has said that his inspiration came from the neighboring Black Forest. Perhaps contemporary architectural trends were also influential. Fritz Leonhardt, one of the world's foremost designers,[33] said that he was impressed by how the project was handled, but he was skeptical about comparing the structural form to that of a tree; the outermost frail branches of a living tree are not intended to withstand heavy loads.

In any case, we are faced with a remarkable piece of man-made "landscape architecture." The slanted roof surface tells us immediately the direction we must take to reach the planes. The tree structures, with their almost Gothic qualities, dominate the space and contrast nicely with the granite-clad floor and terraces. Especially at night, when the powerful uplights literally lift the treetops, the hall emanates a lyrical aura, *eine denkwurdige Eriebnis*.

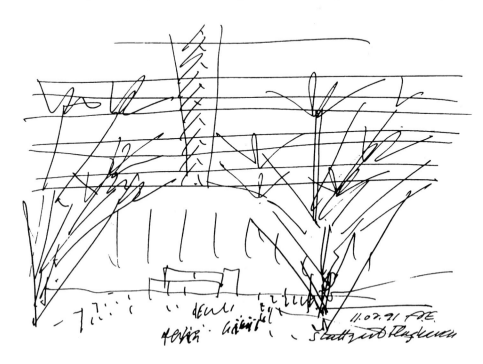

Stuttgart Airport
Architect: Von Gerkan
& Marg

175

Palazzo del Lavoro, Turin

Over the past 150 years, exhibitions have brought us great pioneering structures—the Crystal Palace, built for the world's fair in London in 1851, and Galerie des Machines, erected for the world's fair in Paris in 1889, both discussed earlier in this book. No other building type puts such high demands on flexibility as the exhibition hall. It must be a large spatial unit in which the main overall concept becomes decisive. This gives the architect and the engineer the opportunity to work with the single essential factor needed to make the hall stand—the structure. Because the actual building program is simple—it's only a matter of one large space—other elements will not easily intrude. It is the construction process itself that determines the form and expression the building will take.

Pier Luigi Nervi (1891–1979) is one of this century's great designers, a practical visionary who could design, calculate, and build his own structures. What we associate with him the most are fantastic vaults and cupola structures in concrete. But in the Palazzo del Lavoro from 1961, he demonstrates that he can also master steel as a structural material. The Palazzo del Lavoro was erected in commemoration of the centennial of Italy's unification and the establishment of its

Palazzo del Lavoro,
Turin, 1961
Designer: Pier Luigi
Nervi
Under construction

first parliament in Turin in 1861. It constituted the cornerstone of the exhibition complex on Corso Polonia along the Po River in Turin.

The 158 x 158-meter / 527 x 527-foot hall is dominated by 16 colossal concrete columns, which are 20 m tall and support enormous square steel umbrellas measuring 36 x 36 m / 120 x 120'. Each umbrella is clearly defined at its perimeter by a continuous skylight. The space is also thoroughly illuminated from all four sides through glass facades. The 16 columns of prefabricated concrete were erected in a little under one week. With their strong, cruciform-shaped foundations, they alone ensure the hall's stability. The column shafts end in round capitals, designed to receive the steel umbrellas. The umbrellas consist of a radial arrangement of tapering ribs with stiffeners in plate steel, the bottom flanges of which turn downwards as they approach the column and then converge into the column capital. The steel capital on the concrete column expresses its function of dividing the load just as beautifully and correctly as in a Doric sandstone temple.

The secondary building systems have also found their richly articulated and structurally correct expression. The very high glass facades are braced with vertical steel ribs. Being thicker in the middle, their shapes correspond to the moment diagram of the wind loads. Between these, horizontal *brise soleil* elements are mounted.

The jubilee exhibition is long forgotten, but the hall remains standing, having found its place in the history of architecture. Visitors to the hall today get a very different experience. The large glass facades have not been cleaned since the 1960s. Nervi's famous free-floating mezzanines are encased in plasterboard walls to provide space for the municipal school classes that are held there. Yet the tension between the space and the large structures still remains.

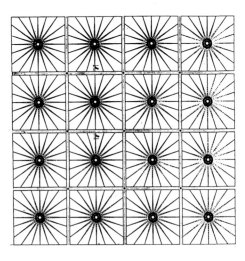

Palazzo del Lavoro,
Turin, 1961
Designer: Pier Luigi
Nervi
Reflected ceiling plan
of the structural system

Palazzo del Lavoro,
Turin, 1961
Designer: Pier Luigi
Nervi
Steel umbrella atop
concrete column

178

Under the Trees of Knowledge

"Under the trees of knowledge" was the motto of the winning design in a competition for a new library in Tonsberg, Norway, submitted by the architectural firm Lunde and Lovseth in collaboration with professor Kristoffer Apeland as technical advisor. The title is an expression of the interdependence between the building's purpose and the means used to realize it—the connection of function to structure—in which the structure's symbolic qualities metaphorically refer to the tree trunks and treetops and delineate the space according to the literary activities going on among them.

The Tonsberg Library is a response to the widespread criticism of the ascetic tendencies of the modernist tradition. There is a lot that meets the eye here, and the visual impressions appeal as much to the heart as to the mind. The kind of rationality that is associated with structural choices, and that has to do with the quest for integrity and understanding of the building process, does not get in the way of designing structures as figural elements that relate more to history than to the distribution of loads. From our modernist heritage, we learned to use contemporary materials in a natural way. Here materials are used in more complex relationships and forms and in a more eloquent manner than what the pioneers of modernism taught us. In a way, this is modernism adapted to the 1990s; the vault and columns can very well be built in steel.

Tonsberg Library,
Tonsberg, 1992
Detail of steel structure

Meanwhile, the clean-cut glass facade doesn't quite match the proportions of the expressive interior. Even if the intention has been to minimize the transition from outside to inside and to expose the steel structure as much as possible, this is best experienced after dusk, when the interior is illuminated. In daylight, the facade's reflections don't provide the desired transparency or the intended experience of a streetscape in a small town.

The library's plan is functionally and characteristically divided into two parts by an arched brick-veneered concrete wall. Behind this wall are the spaces that are not accessible to the public, such as personnel offices. The other part is the large space that is dominated by the beautiful steel structures and that contains the book collection, reading areas, and a small cafe.

Here the roof is supported by the arched steel perforated beams that create characteristic series of vaulted shapes. The arching is not great and has a radius of 5.5 and 8 m / 18 and 26'. Spanning the arched, perforated beams are purlins that are only partially visible and support the corrugated aluminum roof. The undersurface is clad in steel panels coated with aluminum and zinc, which are light in character. The arched beams, in turn, are supported by compression rods 108 mm / 4¼" in diameter that branch into a treetop shape. These are gathered in a striking detail at the top of the column: Crescent-shaped disks receive the steel branches and transport the loads to the columns. Each column has a diameter of about 400 mm / 16" and carries two arched beams via two sets of branches. Each pair of branches from opposite sets is connected by a tension stay that prevents the two from splaying. The columns are braced laterally and at their footings by intermediate decks. Each entire "treetop," that is, the two arched beams and compression struds, is laterally braced by the vaulting roof structure, which is firmly anchored to the arched brick-veneered concrete wall.

The Tonsberg Library stands out as a particularly successful example of architecture in which steel's special advantages and traits were allowed to come into their own, in part because of a close collaboration between architects and engineers. The architects have this to say about this approach: "Today's building technology provides greater possibilities for bold structures. Nevertheless, it is seldomly used as part of a main concept. Perhaps this is because there is no collaboration between engineer and architect in the preliminary phases, or because of the lack of tradition for special structures."[34] The Tonsberg Library bears witness to what good can come of such a collaboration. The building was awarded both the Norwegian and European Steel Construction Prize for 1993.

onsberg Library,
onsberg, 1992
iew of interior from
ntrance

Historic buildings give us the best and most tangible contact with the past. They ar
also fundamentally significant in understanding the relationship of past, present
and future. But it is not enough to merely restore a building to its original state; A
minute "scientific" reconstruction does not necessarily give us the best histori
insight. We may not even want to use the building for what it was originally intende
since we live in different times. The architect Sverre Fehn (born 1924) put it thi
way: "Only with the language of the present can we get the past to speak." I
Hedmark's Museum at Domkirkeodden near Hamar, Norway, we can experience

Hedmarks Museum,
1970
Storhamar barn
Architect: Sverre Fehn
Sigd

history through an architectural stroll along free-floating ramps in one of the materials of our time—reinforced concrete. Stone sculptures for the Middle Ages, old drinking vessels, and other utilitarian objects are presented to the viewer clasped by Fehn's beautiful oil-burned steel fittings.

The National Gallery for the region of Emilia Romagna in northern Italy is in Parma at the Palazzo della Pilotta, an enormous mannerist style building designed by architect Guido Canali (born 1936). Throughout this complex, with its dramatic past marked by fires, accidents, additions, and reconstructions, the collections are arranged along a strictly organized path. The visitor makes his way through alternating spaces and illumination on ramps, bridges, staircases, and through galleries. Massive brick walls and colossal timbers used as beams are impressive symbols of 14th-century power, but in contrast to the rustic masses appear newly introduced steel structures of refined precision. One of the most intriguing elements

Hedmarks Museum,
1970
Storhamar barn
Architect: Sverre Fehn

are the railings with slender, almost under-dimensioned sections. They consist
double banisters, closely spaced and joined at the top by small spacers with sma
hexagonal black bolts that help to anchor the handrail. The horizontal runners
round bar steel are drilled through the banisters. In between, there are fittings wi
suspended decks, supported by white-painted steel, three-dimensional frame
similar to those used in tubular scaffolding. Canali has not tried to weave his wa
into the original building structure. With the new museum installations he define
space with the help of levels and lines—horizontal, vertical, and diagonal. Th
meeting of opposites, of the past and present, of the massive structures an
skeletons, brick and steel, gives richness to Parma's Pilotta.

*Galleria Nazionale del
Palazzo della Pilotta,
Parma
Architect: Guido
Canali
Steel pedestrian bridge*

STEEL IN COMBINATION WITH OTHER MATERIALS

Mound Stand, Lord's
Cricket Ground,
London, 1987
*Architect: Michael
Hopkins & Partners
Engineer: Ove Arup &
Partners*

185

Wood has always been universally used as a building material. Similarly, brick ha been used for a wide range of purposes, particularly in areas surrounding th Mediterranean Sea. Cupolas and vaults also can be found in many kinds of space In a structural context, however, steel is a relatively new material, widesprea applications having only come into usage as late as the nineteenth century. Mo people can't conceive of a building made entirely of steel; a bridge, a ship, course—but not a building. And so it is interesting to look at steel combined wi other materials. After all, one material may not, or need not, possess all th properties required to satisfy every demand placed on a structure. When combine materials of different properties create new forms of architectural expressio engaging in a fresh, meaningful dialogue.

*Pavilion for Fort
Nathan Hale, New
Haven, 1986
Architects: Class of '88,
Yale School of
Architecture*

Steel and Masonry

Through his restoration of some of the most important Gothic buildings in France, Eugene-Emmanuel Viollet-le-Duc (1814–1879) gained an understanding of their basic structure. In traditional building, masonry takes up the greatest volume on the ground floor, where, for functional reasons, most buildings require the largest amount of continuous free space. This led to his theories about combining steel skeletons with masonry structures, such as vaults and cupolas. In his conceptual project for a large hall one can see how the masonry cupolas are literally severed at their abutments. Here, traditional vertical masonry pillars are replaced by tilted compression members in tubular cast-iron that direct the loads out to brackets on the outer walls. Forged tension rods hold the system in balance and prevent the brick walls from being "kicked outward," while the severed cupolas are well supported by the steel structures. The joints are nicely articulated and there is a delicate distinction between elements taking compression and tension loads.

Another of Viollet-le-Duc's famous works is the project for a market hall. The main beams are made of steel and are supported by steel columns. The columns, in pairs, form V shapes that support the spaces above.

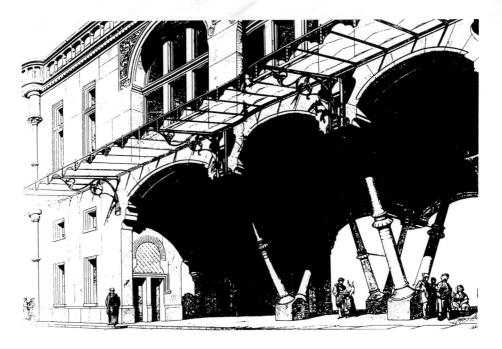

Market hall with room above
Viollet-le-Duc

Through his theoretical studies and projects, Viollet-le-Duc shows that where the traditional building methods fall short, a new material—steel—finds its niche. In our day, with the bewildering number of possible architectural directions, it is interesting to note Viollet-le-Duc's comment (in *Lectures on Architecture*, lecture XII) that architecture cannot find new expressions of form without them being based on new structural methods.

*Interior of a large hall
Viollet-le-Duc*

St. Petri Church in Klippan, Sweden

Designed by the Swedish architect Sigurd Lewerentz (1885–1975), St. Petri Church in Klippan, in the southern Swedish province of Skane, is the realization of some of Viollet-le-Duc's theoretical architectural formulations: Masonry and steel join to form a perfectly harmonized synthesis in which the two materials are used with a profound sensitivity to their natural properties. This respect for the materials' properties—esthetic, craftsmanlike, and structural—is a conspicuous trait of Lewerentz's architecture.

The competence and high quality we find at all levels in St. Petri Church is the result of Lewerentz's meticulous work methods. After an objective analysis of all aspects of the building task, the architect drew each brick and each steel element and made sure to be present at the building site during construction. This shows us the importance of allowing the architect to be the actual building leader, provided he has the ability and inclination to avail himself of this opportunity.

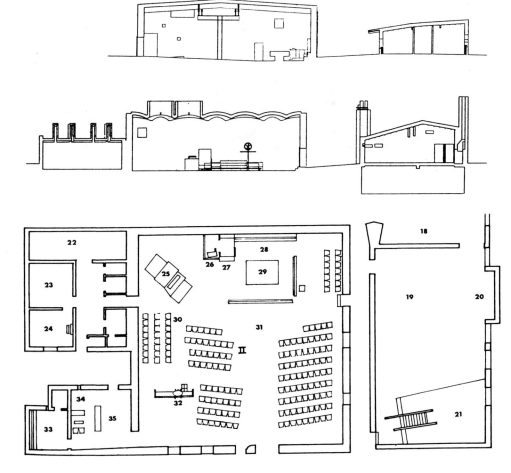

. Petri Church,
'ippan, Skane, 1966
·chitect: Sigurd
·werentz
igineer: Hjalmar
·anholm, Inc.
·ctions

. Petri Church,
'ippan, Skane, 1966
·chitect: Sigurd
·werentz
igineer: Hjalmar
·anholm, Inc.
·oor plan

Spanning the 18 x 18 m / 60 x 60' church space are masonry and steel conic
barrel vaults supported by a single steel column in the middle of the space. T.
steel post forms a T-shaped cross with a cross beam that, in turn, carries two ste
girders across the width of the space. The entire steel structure is made up of pair
single sections to minimize the dimensions. During the building process, Lewerer
allowed the steel sections to lie outside and rust. Afterward, they were steel brush
to acquire a tone well matched to the color of brick.

Sigurd Lewerentz was undeniably interested in technical approaches, and he w
able to coordinate these with craftsmanlike and artistic approaches. This is why
is correct to say that in his architecture the structural and the practical a
inseparable from the esthetic.

St. Petri Church,
Klippan, Skane, 1966
Architect: Sigurd
Lewerentz
Engineer: Hjalmar
Granholm, Inc.
Interior

Steel and Wood

The Norwegian State Railways (NSB) is rebuilding 11 freight centers around the country as part of the replacement and development of its freight division. The Ostfold Freight Center is one of these. The truck garage will house a 42-ton forklift for lifting containers between trains and trucks. Made of standard steel sections with bolted connections, a rigid frame structure with a rectangular ground plan is surrounded by a secondary wall structure of wood with an oval ground plan. The roof surface between the steel structure and this curved outer wall is covered with transparent plastic panels, which provide overhead light in the area used by maintenance personnel. Wind bracing is provided by diagonal tension rods in an X configuration that meet in a steel ring at the center of the X. The tension rods are

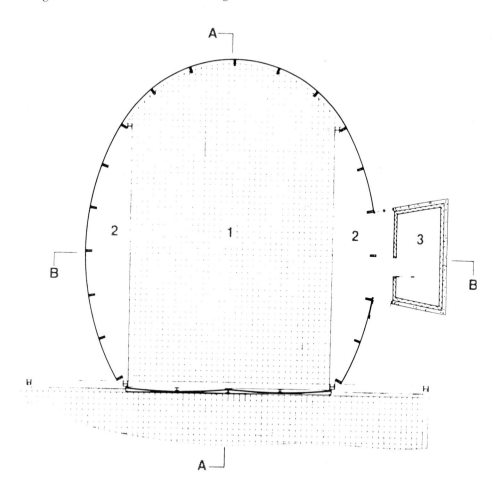

SB Rolvsoy Freight
nter, 1989
chitect: NSB
chitect Office, Jan
av Jensen
gineer: Kristoffer
eland

bolted to the ring. The outer wall is built of laminated wood studs anchored at t[h]e
base and tied to the steel structure above by means of double wooden joists. The[y]
meet the steel girders at different angles, which are reconciled by vertical pipes th[at]
are welded in between the flanges of the steel girders. The laminated wood studs a[re]
spaced at 2 m / 6'6" on center. Because the wall is curved, the single-lay[er]
horizontal siding attains a certain rigidity. The same principle is used in the tw[o]
sliding doors. The doors themselves are completely stiff, but they shake in the[ir]
fitting in strong wind gusts. A goal in this project was to use low-maintenan[ce]
materials and finishes—untreated concrete at the base, galvanized steel for th[e]
main structures, and wood treated with creosote.

*NSB Rolvsoy Freight
Center, 1989
Architect: NSB
Architect Office, Jan
Olav Jensen
Engineer: Kristoffer
Apeland*

Steel and Glass

The rapid development of glass as a building material has inspired architects and engineers to move in new directions. Instead of being traditionally mounted in frames, glass can be bonded or bolted to the bearing structure of steel or other metals. Consequently, large, continuous external glass surfaces can be achieved without the introduction of other materials. Structural sealant glass usually requires a system of connected brackets behind it to assure continuous bonded joints, as in the large pyramid at the Louvre (see page 59). Seen from inside, however, the view is partly obstructed by the supporting structure.

La Villette in Paris represents a milestone in the development of the new structural glass. The main objective of the bay windows in the Musée National des Sciences at Parc La Villette, dating from 1982, was to achieve maximum transparency. The quality of the glass used and the degree of control exerted over the details were crucial to the end result. The architect was Adrien Feinsilber, but the engineer, Peter Rice (1936–1992), played a major role in developing the very demanding detailing of the concept. The designers concluded early that the view to the park would be disturbed if they chose vertical bracing sections, whether they were of steel or pure glass fins. They then chose horizontal cable trusses with special fittings for the glass.

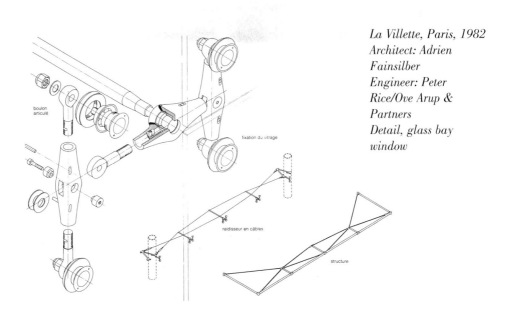

boulon
articulé

fixation du vitrage

raidisseur en câbles

structure

La Villette, Paris, 1982
Architect: Adrien
Fainsilber
Engineer: Peter
Rice/Ove Arup &
Partners
Detail, glass bay
window

The glass is hung like a curtain wall with small vertical brackets fastened to the corners of the glass panes. Bolts are countersunk in the glass so that they lie flush with the outer surface. These elements—in the most precisely executed and highly polished cast stainless steel—are to a large extent picked from catalogues for maritime equipment. Elements such as tension stays and patch fittings come from the rigging of sailboats and yachts. These structures take tension in the same manner as the tension stays in a boat's masts. Here, maritime technology has found an architectural application in the most advanced structural glass systems.

La Villette, Paris, 1982
Architect: Adrien
Fainsilber
Engineer: Peter
Rice/Ove Arup &
Partners
Glass bay window

194

Steel and Fabric

Mound Stand, Lord's Cricket Ground, London

For the British, cricket is as important as baseball is for Americans. Indeed, cricket is in many ways a vital part of their cultural tradition—not only the sport itself, but also the various expectations spectators bring with them to the grandstand. Building a grandstand for cricket's Mecca, therefore, is a task that demanded a great deal of respect and understanding both for the ritual surrounding the sport and the history associated with it. At Mound Stand the British architect Michael Hopkins (born 1948) designed a facility that accomplishes this by using a rich synthesis of different materials, each representing definite structural and visual properties.

Lord's Cricket Ground, London, 1987
Architect: Michael Hopkins and Partners
Engineer: Ove Arup and Partners
Facade facing the street

Lord's Cricket Ground, London, 1987
Uppermost tribune with cover of fabric structures

Facing the street and the city, the grandstand is built with materials that are p[ut] together in hierarchical layers, with heavy masonry as a base for the ste[el] structures, which, in turn, support the light fabric roofs. The masonry arcade, whi[ch] also is new, is a continuation of a corresponding brick structure in another of Lor[d's] grandstands, built in 1899. Its preservation and rehabilitation was an inspir[ed] element of Hopkins' project, and a significant reason behind his having won t[he] architectural competition.

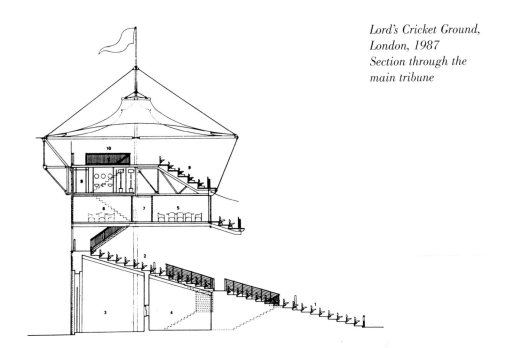

Together with Ove Arup & Partners and engineers Peter Rice and John Thornton, Hopkins erected a steel skeleton that seems to hover above the lowest stand, which is supported by the masonry arcade. The entire upper structure rests on only six steel columns spaced at 18.3 m / 61' on center. The columns are of tubular steel with a diameter of only 406 mm / 16". Between these, at the uppermost level of the stand, steel-plate girders span and run the entire length of the grandstand, serving as a kind of structural spine. Cantilevering from either side of the spine, tapered trussed girder ribs support the upper stand deck and the mezzanine ceiling. To avoid visual barriers like columns among the spectators on the lowest levels, the mezzanine level is suspended by steel rods from the spine girder and ribs above. Along the back of the building, facing the street, there is a deep plate girder, which is one story high and subdivided by stiffeners. This interesting and unusual configuration of a steel-plate girder is exposed and, along with the other materials, constitutes a very beautiful element in the articulation of the facade. This girder runs the entire length of the facade, collecting the out-of-balance loads from the individual beams and transferring them to the steel tie-down rods that prevent the entire grandstand from tipping over. Six columns rise to become masts and from these, the conical fabric roof spans like sails above the upper stand. The fabric used here is made of PVC-coated woven polyester fiber in panels with clamped joints. It is supported by a framework of tubular steel booms and galvanized-steel cables connected to steel rings at the top of each cone, thereby spreading the loads into the material. In combining the steel skeleton with the fabric membrane, Hopkins alludes to the history surrounding the game of cricket, to the days when games were held in tents pitched on a country village's green fields.

Imagination, London

In a 7-meter- / 23-foot-wide slot of backyard that separated two building blocks architect Ron Herron created an outstanding volume with a light quality and character, both visually appealing and functional, as a social and professional gathering space. The owner is the communications firm Imagination, which has rebuilt and converted the space into offices. Light, elegant steel bridges span the new atrium and connect the two buildings at several levels. The bridges and the translucent fabric roof are the main elements of the new design that turns the two buildings and the slot into a unit.

Having considered covering the room with glass, the designers chose to use a roof of stretched fabric. The advantage lies in the material's flexibility, i.e., the ability of the fabric to adapt to a difficult, contorted geometry. A steel skeleton stretches and supports the white cloth made of PVC-coated polyester fiber, while a thin film of acrylic lacquer helps keep the fabric clean. This structural membrane has a translucency of 15%, which creates a well-lighted room without glare. In each 5-meter- / 16-foot-wide structural bay, an umbrellalike structure keeps the fabric in its proper shape and spreads the tension over the entire fabric surface. The

Imagination, London,
1990
Architect: Ron Herron
Associates
Engineer: Buro
Happold
Section

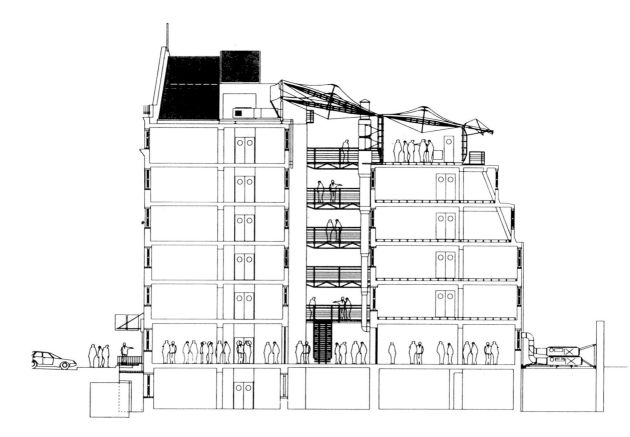

nagination, London,
990
abric surface is
retched by "push-
ps."

umbrellas have nine radiating alloy ribs connected to the top of a tubular aluminum push up rod. Four 12 mm- / ½ " stainless steel tension rods receive the compression forces at the base of the push ups, transmitting them to the four corners of the bay as tension. In turn, these tension forces are transmitted in pairs to the lattice struts that span the room. The tendency for the fabric to become slack with time is compensated by even tautening of the system via turnbuckle connections and by adjusting the length of the vertical push up rods. Buro Happhold, the engineer for this structure and an expert on soft shell structures, developed computer programs for tension analysis and fabric geometry. With the help of such programs, Happold manipulated the fabric's geometry and placement of the "push-ups" until the tension was equalized in such a way as to produce a shape that satisfied the architects.

Imagination, London, 1990
Back courtyard has become an active space.

Steel Details

The basic concepts for large structures may lie in some of the inspired sketches of a Nervi or Utzon, but working out the details, the structural connections, may stretch out over months or years. Peter Rice (1936–1992), one of the engineers behind both the Pompidou Center in Paris and Lloyds of London, points out the difference between what is sketched and what is built. The design of structural links—the pieces—are the result of practical evaluation and testing. The pieces give us the key, the genetic code if you will, to understand how a building stands.

Centre Georges Pompidou, Paris, 1977 Architect: Renzo Piano and Richard Rogers Engineer: Ove Arup Cast-iron anchoring for suspension of interior escalator.

Cruciform Columns

The cruciform steel columns of Mies' Barcelona Pavilion are made of four equal steel T-sections covered with highly-polished chromed sheet steel. The column polished surface is in keeping with the pavilion's other materials—polished, honey yellow onyx, green Tinos marble, and the reflecting glass surfaces. The cruciform section of the columns is neutral in both directions of the orthogonal grid. The alert visitor will notice one change: The chromed columns have been changed to polished stainless steel.

Left: Cruciform steel column in the Barcelona pavilion, 1929.
Architect: Mies van der Rohe
Right: Cruciform steel column in Tugendhat House, Brno, Czechoslovakia, 1930.
Architect: Mies van der Rohe

After the Barcelona Pavilion Mies designed the Tugendhat House in Brno, Czechoslovakia, in 1930. Here, just as he did in Barcelona, Mies demonstrates his ideas about the free plan and the clear construction. The house, which has been restored, is known especially for its open and sober lounge with glass in three of its facades. As in the Barcelona Pavilion, the flat roof is carried by cruciform steel columns. Here, however, the polished sheathing is more rounded. Perhaps the

202

reflects the curved forms found elsewhere in the house—the arched glass wall that surrounds the staircase descending from the entrance terrace and the semicircular screen wall in the lounge.

Le Corbusier's (1887–1965) material of choice was concrete, with its rich plastic potential for expression. However, in his very last work, the Centre Le Corbusier in Zurich from 1967 which was inaugurated after his death, he uses steel as a building material. An umbrellalike sheet-metal construction covers a light pavilion based on cubic volume units measuring 226 x 226 x 226 cm / $7\frac{1}{2}$ x $7\frac{1}{2}$ x $7\frac{1}{2}$' constructed of steel members with a cruciform cross section. In contrast with Mies' free-standing columns, Le Corbusier's cruciform sections are used both horizontally and vertically to define the pavilion's volumes and to frame the facade elements of glass and enameled steel panels. Here there is no sheathing of the cruciform elements. Instead, there are visible connections between the four equal steel angles.

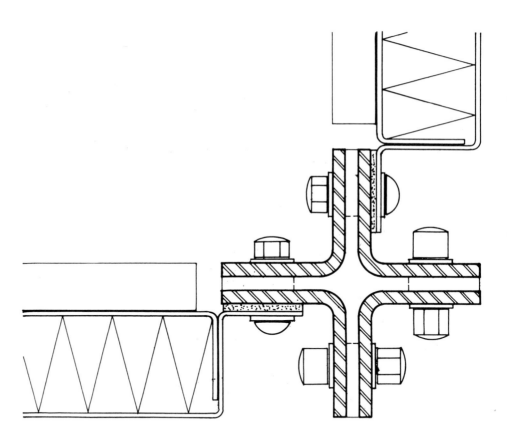

Cruciform steel column in Centre Le Corbusier, Zurich, 1967.
Architect: Le Corbusier

Frame Corners

A frame is a column and beam structure that forms a rigid, static entity. The joined action of all parts of the frame resists both horizontal and vertical loads. If a frame corner is unchangeable in form, bending deflections in the column will be transferred to the beam and vice versa, i.e., they distribute the load between themselves. A rigid frame corner is, in other words, a column-beam connection that keeps its shape, maintaining its corner angle even if the structural elements are loaded and deformed. A right-angled corner will remain right-angled, but will get planar angular displacement. Stable frame structures can also contain hinged or pin connections in which the column and beam can move in relation to one another. A frame can only have three pin joints if it is to remain stable.

The frame has been utilized in countless projects. Here it will suffice to mention two examples in which this structural form is the architectural expression of the building. Defining the actual frame corner in these cases becomes of decisive importance.

Crown Hall at the Illinois Institute of Technology (IIT) in Chicago, dating from 1956, is one of Mies van der Rohe's main works. The building's main plan, which contains the architecture and planning division, consists of a column-free space measuring 40 x 75 m / 133 x 250'. Steel frames make up the primary structural system. The roof is composed of suspended plate girders in the form of deep I-beam sections, with the web strengthened by stiffeners along the entire length beam. The plate girders are supported by external columns of W-sections; together they form the primary frames. The choice of structure calls for rigid frame corners because bracing cannot be accommodated elsewhere in the building. The plate girder and column have the same flange width, and the joints are welded horizontally and vertically so that the flanges of columns and beam can cross each other and achieve a very stiff connection. Thereby the problem has found a simple, but important solution.

*Crown Hall, Illinois
Institute of Technology,
Chicago, 1956
Architect: Mies van der
Rohe*

Norman Foster's (born 1935) 1991 expansion of the Sackler Galleries of the Royal Academy in London was an unusual undertaking for him. In a narrow space between two existing buildings, he designed an impressive architectural work with a gentle touch of restoration. The technical virtuosity for which he is known is subdued here, but nonetheless absolutely present. You have only to look at the roof of the new space, glazed in white transparent Czechoslovakian glass. The primary structure consists of frames that span between the two buildings, so that bracing is provided by the mass of the existing buildings. The frame corners can therefore be hinged. Thus, the frames can take the movement of the beam under load without transferring bending moments to the column. This is a beautiful and accurate detail that grows out of the structural conditions of the building.

Sackler Galleries, Royal Academy, London
Architect: Foster Associates
What material other than steel could recreate the classic calm surrounding this row of sculptures.

206

Mechanical Wood Connectors

The use of wood as a structural material is to a large extent dependent on the right types of connections and on their effectiveness. Development in this area has been of decisive importance to the choice of structural systems. For instance, mechanical connections facilitate the assembly of large wood truss structures, and the use of sheet-metal plates laid the groundwork for a simple and reasonable roof truss production. Currently, the most common mechanical means for connecting wood are nails, bolts, dowels, wood screws, timber connectors, sheet-metal plates, and power driven studs. The common ground for all of these is that they are made of steel.

A particularly interesting timber connector is the toothed ring, also called "bulldog." These are made of sheet-metal, are round or square, one-sided or two-sided, with teeth on the edges that bite into the wood when two pieces are joined. Like the mouse trap and cheese slicer, it is a good, practical Norwegian invention. The inventor, engineer Olav Trygve Theodorsen, received his patent in 1920.

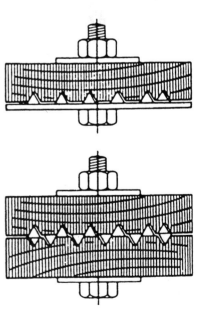

One-sided and two-sided Bulldog

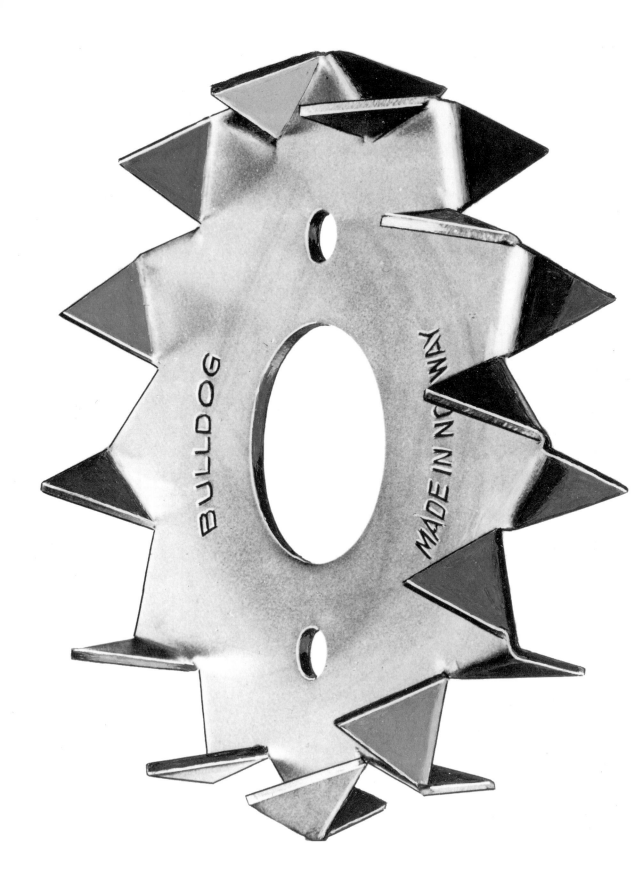

208

26 Sloane Street

The collaboration between architect Eva Jiricna and client Joseph Ettedgui has produced a series of distinguished boutique interiors in London that have aroused the interest of the international design community. Jiricna and Ettedgui are emigrants, from Czechoslovakia and Morocco, respectively. Jiricna's background is as an engineer and architect in Prague. He received a typical East Bloc education in which architectural training is based on previous study of engineering courses, such as statics and construction. An important source of inspiration has been the keen Czech functionalism of the period between the world wars, characterized by light polished surfaces of glass or chrome. Ettedgui had the idea that clothing, furniture, and food should be considered, arranged, and presented as an entity; many would refer to his belief as a life style. The collaboration between the two started with the Joseph Pour La Maison store (1984) at 26 Sloane Street. Here Ettedgui wanted to sell both clothes and furniture, while at the same time setting aside space for a little restaurant. With a monochrome color scheme—black steel ceiling panels, cream-colored floor tiles, display arrangements in glass and stainless steel, and a rare intensity in carrying out every detail—Jiricna created a work with style and a degree of perfection that corresponded to the owner's ideas.

For the boutique at 77 Fulham Road (1988), Ettudgui asked Jiricna to create an atmosphere that combined an Italian palazzo with Eileen Gray.[35] However, no Italian palace has ever had such a staircase. Steps of sand-blasted glass are lighted from above and look as if they are free-floating. The steps are supported at mid-point by circular compression pads that are laterally braced by thin compression struts. The struts are connected to delicate stainless steel trusses that work as stringers. The entire system is hung from struts that connect the stringers to the edges of the slab above, and stabilized by tension members stretching to the floor below. The railing is especially beautiful, constructed in an apparently simple manner with split balusters and tempered glass. With the transparency of the glass and the polished stainless steel, the staircase controls the space without being overpowering—an impressive piece of designing and engineering art.

*Joseph, 77 Fulham
Road, 1988
Architect: Eva Jiricna*

But the staircase must still be regarded as a preliminary study, a "finger exercise" for the ambitious masterwork in their next project, 26 Sloane Street in London. This staircase is a balancing act, with two long runs through three floors and all structural joints reduced to a minimum. The introduction of landings, which often complicates the design of stringers and railings, makes the staircase even more impressive. Quite often, architects prefer designing straight-run stairs. Here the supports are concentrated around the landings with vertical and diagonal struts. The railings are split to minimize their cross section. The main stringer joints are custom designed spheres with "Saturn rings" fastened to numerous tension strut clevises. The free-floating character of the staircase and its glittering precision was the result of Jiricna's collaboration with the engineer Matthew Wells. Concept and detailing are based on structural insight with precise calculations for every point. Jiricna's ability to inspire everyone involved to do their best throughout planning and production also was conducive to a positive end result.

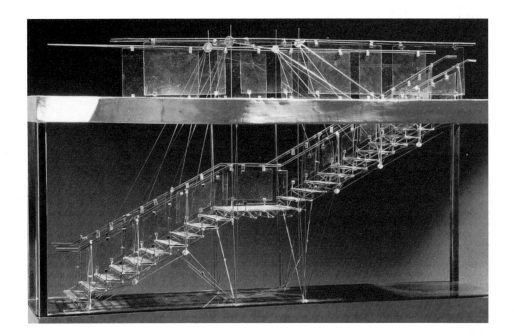

Joseph, 26 Sloane Street, 1989
Architect: Eva Jiricna
Model by Frank Kristiansen

AJ Service

The Danish architect Arne Jacobsen (1902–1971) is the creator of a series of products in stainless steel, the Cylinda line. Based on the idea of utilizing taut cylindrical forms, Jacobsen insisted on the use of seamless tubes with perfectly brushed surfaces. The clear geometric forms and functional, precise design were realized by the manufacturer, Stelton, based on a specially developed technology supplied by computer-controlled pressing machines and laser-cutting machines. A large salad bowl joining an outer cylinder and an inner spherical shape is an especially magnificent piece.

*Cylinda line, Stelton
Design: Arne Jacobsen,
Stelton of Denmark*

Queensboro Bridge,
1909
Engineer: Gustav
Lindenthal.
Architect: Palmer &
Hornbostel.
This bridge was built
almost entirely out of
riveted and bolted
standard steel
elements.

BRIDGES

Pont des Arts, Paris,
1803
*Engineers: Louis
Alexandre Cessart and
Jacques Lacroix-Dillon*

215

Bridge Esthetics

From Sandvika, *1885*
Claude Monet

Several of Claude Monet's (1840–1926) landscape motifs were inspired by th
winter months he spent in Norway in 1895. The motif is dominated by the typica
Norwegian wooden buildings, depicted in Monet's characteristic pastel colors. I
the foreground of *From Sandvika*, the actual core of the composition is Lokk
Bridge, Norway's first cast-iron bridge from Baerum Works, built in 1828. You ca
search in vain for this motif today. Sandvika has changed, the buildings are gon
and the bridge has been moved to another site by Sandviks River. But reminders
how Sandvika once looked remain alive in Monet's pictures, and perhaps it i
mainly the bridge that characterized the site and gave it its identity.

Bridges are essential to every community, and often they dominate the landscape
When we think of a particular place, it is frequently a bridge we see first—th
bridge over the River Kwai, or the Golden Gate Bridge in San Francisco. Bridge

can also have a special significance and symbolic value for historical events—the battle at the bridge in Arnheim, Holland, during World War II described in the novel *A Bridge Too Far*[36]—or bridges can be the connecting link between continents—the bridge over the Bosporus. Bridges also represent some of the most notable infrastructural elements in modern society. Since time immemorial, bridges have served as links between population groups and societies, spanning natural barriers and other obstacles, as the cornerstones of communication and development. Bridges can serve as indicators of a society's state of cultural and/or technical development, and in the consciousness of many people bridges and bridge building are expressions of the best engineering art in modern civilization, in effect tangible barometers of the state of the structural art of the period in which they were created.

The function of the bridge is simple: to bring people and vehicles from one side to another. Structures that are suited for large spans will tend to be simple, logical, and beautiful, almost obvious, clear responses to the dimensioning forces. This is why bridges are usually pure in their artistic style, without unnecessary camouflage or adornment. A bridge's form follows its structure, and its development is the work of the engineer and the builder.

kke Bridge,
ndvika

Baerum Works

nt de Tolbiak, Paris
rom the drawing
ries Brouillard au
nt de Tolbiak
alet and Tardi

During the past decade the tendency has been to get the most bridge for the money. Projects were based solely on the "bottom line," ignoring a multitude of other factors, including the landscape and the environment. This attitude is about to change. In planning large bridge projects in Denmark, for instance, architects and landscape architects have been working together from the early conceptual phase, to ensure the most correct, responsible use of a given site. Even in the details of a bridge's various elements—towers, railings, abutments, etc.—the architect's contribution has begun to make a visible difference. Norway's directory of roads has also become involved in developing bridge esthetics, and is now calling for cooperation among architects, landscape architects, and bridge builders in regard to larger bridge projects. Courses in bridge design, with emphasis on structural as well as environmental concerns, are finding their place in the curriculums of many architecture schools.

Steel Bridges

Long-span bridges are primarily constructed in steel. For many years steel has been produced according to standards that ensure a reliable, homogeneous produce Modern steel combines high strength with other valuable properties that enable the material to meet the broadest, most difficult challenges—an element that made it a indispensible for bridge building in the past as in the present.

The building of steel bridges has a history of about 200 years, starting with the Industrial Revolution in England and the construction of the first purely steel bridge—Ironbridge—across the Severn River near Coalbrooksdale in 1779. But the development of steel bridges gathered real momentum during the past century. pioneering work was the suspension bridge over Menai Strait from Wales to the island of Anglesey, built by the Scot Thomas Telford (1757–1834), one of the great engineers of his day. The railroad bridge across the Firth of Forth, with its 300 meter-long cantilever, was open in 1890 and was long considered to be one of the greatest bridges in the world.

Suspension bridges have their clear, easily understandable logic. A great advantage of suspension bridges over other bridge types is that they don't require scaffolding that has to rest on costly temporary foundations. Over large spans suspension bridges are superior to all other kinds of bridges because the weight of the bridge itself and the live loads are absorbed by cables and other tension members. The rusty-red Golden Gate Bridge in San Francisco, dating from 1930, was for many years the world's longest suspension bridge. The record was beaten long ago, but the Golden Gate remains the "Goddess" of all suspension bridges.

A multi-strut bridge is a variation of a suspension bridge. It can be asymmetrical with one tower or several towers of different heights. Large multi-strut bridges are prominent landmarks on the road between the German cities of Hamburg and Cologne.

In Norway, where bridging over beautiful fjords and mountain passes is indispensable, bridge building is an integral part of railroad construction. The bridge office of the Norwegian State Railways has built a great number of interesting steel bridges, like the Askoy Bridge. With a span of 850 m / 2,850', it is the longest suspension bridge in the Nordic countries.

Facing page: Bridge across Firth of Forth, 1890
Designers: Benjamin Baker and John Fowler
Trussed bridge with riveted steel members
Span 521 m / 1,737'

Ironbridge

*Ironbridge across the
Severn, 1779
In calm weather the
bridge and its
reflection form a
perfect circle.*

The first bridge made of iron was built in 1779 across the Severn River in England, at a site that later was to be called Ironbridge. In this part of the English Midlands, the Darby family dynasty produced iron based on coke instead of charcoal, establishing the foundation for the first industrial products manufactured from iron. The bridge's cast-iron elements were manufactured at Abraham Darby's ironworks according to instructions from the architect, Thomas Farnolls Pritchard, and the engineer, John Wilkinson. The concept, which is based on a semicircle, derives several of its features from the traditional, craftsmanlike bridges built of wood and stone, perhaps reminiscent of those made of logs by the Swiss. But the bridge can also be seen as an arch of wedge shapes, like arched bridges built of chiseled stone. What separates this bridge from those that preceeded it, however, is that its entire structure is made of iron, put together with the largest elements that could be cast at that time—quater circles for the arches and straight rods that joined them.

In retrospect it is easy to see the weak points in its construction. Only one of the arches is continuous, while the two others die on the underside of the bridge deck. In addition, some of the ornamentation is, strictly speaking, non-structural. Today, the landmarked Ironbridge is still in use as a pedestrian bridge and, with its 100-foot span and graphite-treated arches and rods, stands beautifully amid the river landscape. In calm weather the bridge arch and its reflection in the water form a perfect circle.

Ironbridge

Pont des Arts

His genius was in understanding that iron, above all other materials, could span two riverbanks without breaking the plane of the water.

—of the bridge's engineer, Louis-Alexandre de Cessart[38]

Pont des Arts, Paris, 1803
Engineer: Louis-Alexandre de Cessart and Jacques Lacroix-Dillon

Possessing a strong interest in the English methods[39] and further inspired by the iron bridge at Coalbrookdale, the aging engineer Louis-Alexandre de Cessart (1719–1806) designed the bridge over the Seine, from the Louvre toward the Ecole des Beaux-Arts. The bridge, completed in 1803, was the first successful cast-iron bridge to be built in France. The foot bridge, *Pont des Arts,* in the heart of Paris in a district that was historic even in 1803, makes it possible to cross the Seine on foot in a real panoramic promenade.

To have introduced a new building material in such surroundings is a remarkable achievement, particularly for a man who in 1800 was 81 years old. Napoleon Bonaparte had little confidence in the new bridge and thought it a wretched structure. But de Cessart proceeded, designing the bridge like a building framework in iron. He had originally intended to make the piers out of wood, but when the project was entrusted to another engineer, Jacques Lacroix-Dillon (1760–1807), a professor at Ecole Polytechnique, the piers were changed to stone. Lacroix-Dillon also made other modifications that resulted in the structure we see today, albeit it in a rebuilt form.

Pont des Arts connects the two Seine shores with the help of nine arch spans, each measuring 18.5 m / 62'. Each span is built with five arches cast in two halves and riveted together at the top of the arch. There are iron stiffeners between the arches that make the width of the bridge one unified structure. Furthermore, the arches are stiffened with straight and curved cast-iron members at each pier, a structural detail that softens the linear look of the bridge, as if each arch readies itself for the next span before the previous one is complete. The actual bridge deck is clad in hard wood.

This old iron bridge is a source of inspiration even today, with its design that complements the structural properties and potential of the material. The structure's unity is preserved in its construction, as well as in the railings and lampposts.

Norwegian State Railways' Hinged-Pillar Viaducts

Hoems Bridge with the Graakal railway, Trondheim
One of NSB's original hinged-pillar viaducts

Bridges are an important part of the Norwegian railway network. Norway has 2,700 railway bridges, most of then shorter than 10 meters. It is the few larger bridges however, that one notices and remembers. During the 1870s, NSR introduced a new type of bridge, the hinged-pillar viaduct, which aroused a great deal of attention well beyond Norway's borders. Even today the hinged-pillar viaduct is used as the boilerplate for NSR's many viaducts. The bridge was divided into a number of spans supported by hinged-pillars, frames with hinged joints at the top and bottom. An individual span was comprised of two parallel trusses with arched bottom chords. The trusses function as moment beams, the depths of which conformed to their moment. The hinged structure absorbed unforeseen settling in the foundation without transmitting moments. This type of bridge was well suited for prefabrication as it was easy to assemble with relatively few structural elements.

One of these bridges, the Hoems Bridge, still standing in Trondheim, is noteworthy for its many fine details in steel and the beauty of its surrounding countryside. Hinged-pillars and trusses are executed in riveted steel sections with effective diagonal bracing. All joints are fully exposed. The hinged joints, cast-iron cylindrical bearings, are a good example of a fine engineering tradition.

As trains became heavier and speeds increased, this type of bridge proved lacking in strength. For some time the trusses were reinforced on the sides with iron plates and thus functioned as plate girders. Eventually, the hinged-pillar viaducts were torn down and gradually replaced by other types of bridges.

ems Bridge,
ondheim
linder bearings for
nged-pillar

Building a Bridge in Denmark

The Danish art of bridge construction is internationally renowned. Since the turn of the century, Danish companies have made their mark on five continents. During the 1960s, a firm like Christiani & Nielsen had 17,000 employees and numerous projects for roads, railroads, and bridges. Their influence was so widespread that many of Denmark's engineers received their training at foreign affiliates of Christiani & Nielsen.

Today Denmark has four large steel bridges. (A fifth bridge, over Storebaelt, is currently under construction.) They are completely different from one another and each one illustrates some of the best features of its category. Both of Denmark's principal waterways—Lillebaelt and Storstrommen—are spanned by bridges

The new Lillebaelts Bridge from 1970 connects Fyn and Jutland
Architect: Hvidt & Molgard-Nielsen
Engineer: Cowiconsult, Inc.

Combined vehicle and railroad bridges were built during the 1930s; the next generation built highway bridges.

The old Lillebaelt Bridge from 1935 allows passage of a railroad track and two narrow vehicle lanes along five large spans. The bridge is built like a truss with a rectangular cross section. The two side trusses carry the vertical loads while two trusses lying horizontally above and below the deck surface take the wind loads. Assembly of the steel trusses was an exciting process that captured the public's attention for months. The deck was built simultaneously for both sides from each foundation with 100 m / 333' cantilever projections before they reached the corresponding sections of the neighboring foundation.

The new suspension bridge over Lillebaelt between Fyn and Jylland was constructed like a classic suspension bridge in 1970. The design by the engineering company Cowiconsult A/S and architects Hvidt & Molgaard-Nielsen allowed for a less complicated production and assembly of elements, industrial prefabrication, and steady work rhythm. All of steel's positive properties were utilized to the maximum benefit. The bridge's deck is built as a welded steel box with a sharp, aerodynamic cross section, designed to withstand wind loads.

Below: The new Lillebaelt Bridge suspension cables with adjustable connection

Right: The new Lillebaelt Bridge inside the anchor block the main cable is controlled by a collar mounted on a movable fitting.

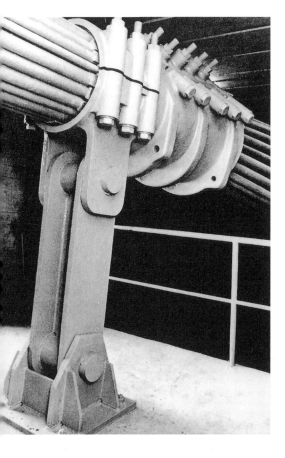

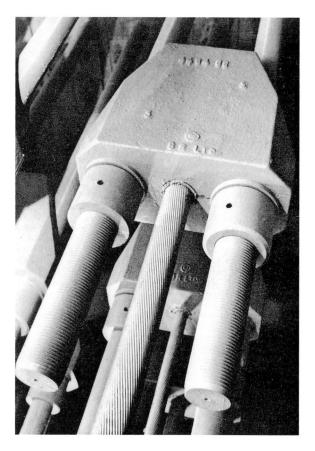

The Storstrommen Bridge, spanning between Sjaelland and Falster, is an honest-to-goodness arch bridge built in steel for vehicles and trains. It was built around the same time as the old Lillebaelt Bridge. A few kilometers away are the new Faro bridges, designed by the engineering firms Cowiconsult A/S and Christiani & Nielsen A/S in collaboration with architect E. Villefrance. It is important to note that the deck does not rest on the horizontal members of the towers, but is suspended freely from diagonal stays. In this flat landscape the beautiful configuration of the Faro bridge's tower is a striking site.

The Faro bridges between Sjaelland and Falster, 1985 Engineer: Chriatiani & Nielsen, Inc. The design of the bridge called for a hollow steel deck that would hang freely from cables without resting on the cross beams.

A Bridge Can Be a Place

Architecture schools around the world are following Santiago Calatrava's bridge projects with increasing interest. His remarkable ability to unite form and structure is having a marked influence on many student projects.

Creteil is a new suburb of Paris at the juncture of the Marne and Seine rivers. Along the river banks people ask in vain about Calatrava's *passerelle*, the pedestrian bridge built in 1988. One usually thinks of a bridge in relation to water, spanning a river, for instance. But like his famous bridge Bach de Rode-Felipe II in Barcelona, this bridge spans no river—only the highway between Paris and Bonneuil.

The concept behind this light, elegant bridge is based on an arch with two pipes leaning symmetrically against each other and joined by steel-plate triangles. The convex form of the bridge's deck, widest in the middle, is suspended by cables from the two arches. The details, railings, suspended cables—all so important to the overall impression—are precisely and beautifully designed, all in white-painted steel. From below the bridge is extremely beautiful in its organic design, almost like a bleached whale skeleton.

destrian bridge at
eteil, Paris, 1988
ntiago Calatrava
del by Benedicte
ercke, Liv Aimee
lvorsen, Lise
rstuvold and
roline Stovring

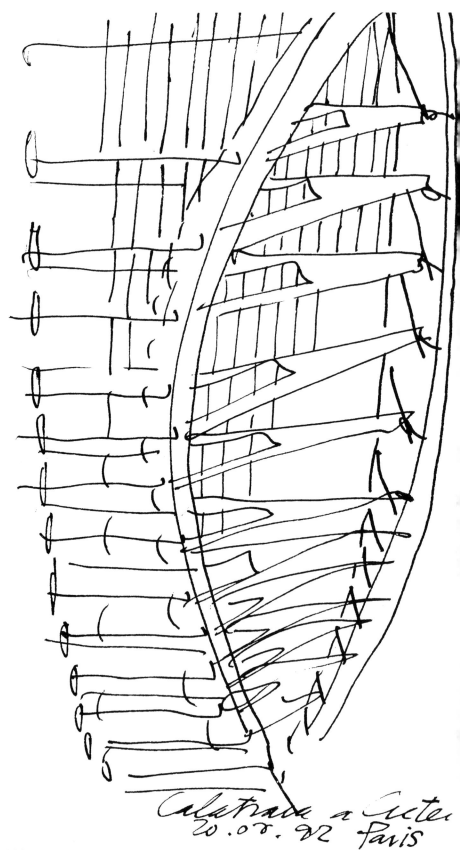

Santiago Calatrava,
Pedestrian bridge at
Creteil, Paris, 1988
Underside of bridge

230

The world's fair in Seville, Expo-92, resulted not only in large-scale building at the exhibition site but in a welcomed opportunity to rejuvenate the entire infrastructure of the city—roads, airports, and railway stations. One of the most prominent buildings in this category is Puente del Alamillo, which joins central Seville with the northern part of the exhibition site. The bridge, designed by Santiago Calatrava, consists of a gigantic slanted concrete pillar wrapped in steel formwork from which 13 pairs of cables stretch to support the bridge deck. With his occasional predilection for musical metaphors, Calatrava has given Seville a harp of divine proportions. The bridge stands as a landmark in the city, and will perhaps become as symbolic of Seville as the Eiffel Tower (built for the world's fair in 1889) is of Paris.

The structural concept allowed Calatrava to reduce the depth of the deck to a minimum so that the bridge appears as a thin line drawn over the Quadalquiver River. Caltrava separated the vehicular from the pedestrian traffic by having vehicles from both directions use the outer edges of the bridge while pedestrians safely use the middle. The pedestrian walkway is also elevated above the vehicular traffic affording an unobstructed view of the surroundings. The pedestrian walkway is really an enormous steel box girder with great resistance to torsion loads from the vehicular lanes cantilevering from it. Also typical of Calatrava is his treatment of the terrain beneath the bridge near its landings. He has devoted considerable effort to making the bridge a total design entity, a pleasant place to be in and look at.

Puente del Alamillo,
Seville, 1992
Santiago Calatrava

The Askoy Bridge

The press coverage for the joining of the two halves of the bridge deck was very enthusiastic. As one paper put it: "It isn't every day that the cultural landscape acquires such beautiful and grandiose lines as when the steel sculptor joined Askoy and Bergen together."[40] When you arrive by sea the bridge appears as an imposing portal over Byfjorden on your way into Bergen harbor. After 30 years of planning and parliamentary debate, one of the island municipalities, Askoy, finally got the bridge connection to the mainland that it longed for.

The bridge deck is built like a closed, totally welded steel box with an aerodynamic cross section according to known guidelines from such structures as the Severn Bridge in England, dating from the mid–1960s, and the Lillebaelt Bridge in

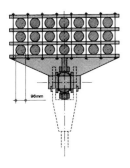

*The Askoy Bridge
Main cable consists of
21 cord sections.*

Denmark, mentioned earlier in this chapter. The steel deck is divided lengthwise
into bulkheads separated by transverse girders, one every 4 m / 13'. The distance
between suspension rods is 12 m / 40'. Corrosion protection consists of galvanized
zinc spray and subsequent painting, yet the deck's interior surface was left
untreated because a dehumidifying system ensures that the relative humidity does
not exceed 40%.

The steel deck sections, which were completed at a shipyard in Ostfold, were
transported by barge to the bridge site and lifted into place by crane. The two cable
bundles are made of prefabricated, fully galvanized individual cables 99 mm / 3⅞"
in diameter. Each bundle consists of 21 such cables. An individual cable has a
guaranteed breaking load capacity of 9060kN and weighs about 71 tons.

The 150 meter- / 500-foot towers are shaped like frame structures with pillars cast
in concrete built with sliding formwork. All of the steel, deck, and suspension cables
are painted dark blue. The towers and viaducts are in untreated concrete. Some
figures provide an idea of the dimensions of this imposing structure: the free span
850 m / 2,835', total length 1,057 m / 3,525' and the steel weight of the deck is 4,200
tons. The bridge's most characteristic feature is its deck with its sharply defined
airplane-wing cross-section and its resilient longitudinal curvature.

*The Askoy Bridge
Section of bridge deck
prepared for transport*

234

Askoybrua 11·08·?2

235

NOTES

1. Chemetov and Marrey, *Architectures à Paris 1848–1914,* 15.

2. Elias, *Building Techniques,* 200.

3. Chemetov and Marrey, *Architectures à Paris 1848–1914,* 188.

4. Ibid., 28.

5. Ibid., 39.

6. Ibid., 28.

7. Ibid., 123.

8. *Architectural Teaching Programme,* section 2, 1.

9. For further descriptions and definitions, see Sandaker and Eggen, *The Structural Basis of Architecture,* 54ff.

10. Ibid., 116ff.

11. Benjamin, *Paris: Capital City of the 1800s,* vol. 1, 7.

12. Geist, *Arcades.*

13. Brodtkorb, *Byggekunst,* No. 4/1991.

14. Sudjic, *Nine Projects Japan,* 6.

15. Ibid., 19.

16. Gans, *Bridging the Gap,* 150.

17. Fordy, *The Architectural Review,* "Art Center, Yale University," 39.

18. Norberg-Schulz, *Meaning in Western Architecture,* 178.

19. Ibid., 178.

20. Chemetov and Marrey, 187.

21. Frampton, *Modern Architecture: A Critical History,* 35.

22. Giedion, *Space, Time and Architecture,* 271.

23. Ibid., 274.

24. Wilkinson, *Supersheds*, 7.

25. *Architectural Review*, December/1989, 42.

26. *Byggekunst*, No. 1/2/1991, 26

27. Davies, *British Pavillion, Seville Exposition 1992*.

28. Ibid.

29. Ahronov and Kent, *High Tech: Craft and Caro*, 21.

30. Hilton, *On Caro's Later Work*, 68.

31. Fenton, *Anthony Caro*, 17.

32. Hilton, *On Caro's Later Work*, 71.

33. In connection with Fritz Leonhardt's lecture on bridge esthetics in the Oslo Architect's Society, November 3, 1993.

34. Lunde and Lovseth, *Cross Section of a Moment*, "Interpretation of Place and Function," 44.

35. Eileen Gray (1878–1976): Irish/English architect and designer who worked in Paris for almost 70 years. Especially known for her furniture and interior designs in the international style.

36. Ryan, *A Bridge Too Far*. London: Coronet Books, 1985.

37. Chemetov and Marrey, *Architectures à Paris 1848–1914*, 14.

38. Ibid., 14.

39. *Bergens Tidende*, April 6, 1992.

40. Ibid.

BIBLIOGRAPHY

Iron, Architecture, and History

Chemetov, Paul and Marrey, Bernard. *Architectures à Paris*. Paris: Dunod, 1984.

Cornell, Elias. *Building Techniques, 2nd edition*. Byggförlaget, 1979.

Steel, The Process and the Product

Architectural Teaching Programme, section 2. "Steel Technology." British Steel.

Orton, Andrew. *The Way We Build Now*. Workingham: Van Nostrand Reinhold, 1988.

Romstad, Håkon (editor). *Steel Handbook, Part 2*. Oslo: Ingeniorforlaget, 1971.

Sandaker B., Eggen, A. *Architecture's Structural Foundations*, 2nd edition. Oslo: Cappelen Fakta, 1991.

The Steel Building Institute. *Steel Building*, Publication 130. 1991

Thrane, Esben. *Steel and Steel Structures: Lectures at AHO and NTH*. Oslo: The College of Architecture, 1981.

Glazed Spaces

Benjamin, Walter. *Paris, the Capital of the 19th Century: The Passage Works*. Stockholm/Stehag: Symposium Publishers, 1990.

Hartung, Giselher. *The Iron Construction of the 19th Century*. Munich: Schirmer/Mosel, 1983.

Hennig-Schefold, Monica and Schmidt-Thomsen, Helga. *Transparency and Mass: The Passage and Hall of Iron and Glass 1800–1880*. Cologne: M. DuMont Schauberg Publishers, 1972.

Blaser, Werner. *Filigree Architecture*. Basel/New York: Wepf & Co., 1980.

Kohlmaier, Georg and von Sartory, Barna. *Houses of Glass, a Nineteenth-Century Building Type*. Cambridge, Massachusetts/London: MIT Press, 1986.

Geist, J.F. *Arcades*. Cambridge: MIT Press, 1983.

Dansk Arkitektur, No. 4: 1980.

Carlson, Per-Olof. *Glass, the Building Material with Possibilities.* Stockholm: The Building Research Council, 1992.

Theme: Forge and Cast Iron and Steel

Geerlings, Gerald K. *Wrought Iron in Architecture: An Illustrated Survey.* New York: Dover Publications Inc., 1959.

Romstad, Håkon (editor). *Steel Handbook, Part 2.* Oslo: Ingeniorforlaget, 1971.

Betschart, A.P. *New Construction in Architecture.* Stuttgart: Institute for the Development of Design and Building Techniques, 1985.

Architectural Teaching Programme, section 2. "Steel Technology." British Steel.

Guedes, Pedro (editor). *The Macmillan Encyclopedia of Architecture and Technological Change.* London/Basingstoke: The Macmillan Press, 1979.

Gale, W.K.V. *Iron and Steel.* The Ironbridge Gorge Museum Trust, 1979.

Piano, R. and Rogers, R. *Du Plateau Beaubourg au Centre Georges Pompidou.* Paris: Editions du Centre Pompidou, 1987.

Multi-Storied Buildings

Hart, F., Henn, W., and Sontag, H. *Multi-Storey Buildings in Steel,* 2nd edition. Cambridge University Press, 1985.

Steel Building Institute. *Steel Building,* SBI publication No. 130, 2nd edition. Stockholm: 1991.

Hill, A., Tidemann, S., and Aasen, B. *Modern Building in Steel Construction.* Oslo/Gol: Norwegian Society of Civil Engineers, 1987.

Byggekunst, No. 4. "Building Research Series: Building Details," Vol I-III. Norwegian Institute of Building Research, 1991.

Sudjic, Deyan. *Nine Projects Japan: Richard Rogers Partnership for K-One Corporation and Mitsubishi.* London: Blueprint Extra 03, 1991.

Brooks, Alan and Grech, Chris. *Connections: Studies in Building Assembly.* Oxford: Butterworth-Heinemann Ltd., 1992.

Gans, Deborah. *Bridging the Gap.* New York: Van Nostrand Reinhold, 1991.

Theme: Surface Treatment and Corrosion Prevention

Romstad, Håkon (editor). Steel Handbook. Oslo: Ingeniorforlaget, 1971.

Architectural Teaching Program, section 2. "Steel Technology." British Steel.

Thrane, Esben. *Steel and Steel Structures: Lectures at AHO and NTH.* Oslo: The College of Architecture, 1981.

Spade, Rupert. *Eero Saarinen.* London: Thames and Hudson, 1971.

Jotun Protective Coatings. *Painting Handbook.* Sandefjord, 1989.

Architectural Record, May 1985.

Prown, Jules David. *The Architecture of the Yale Center of British Art.* New Haven: Yale University, 1977.

Brownlee, David B. *Louis I. Kahn.*

De Long, David G. *In the Realm of Architecture.* New York: Rizzoli, 1991.

Wide-Span Single-Story Buildings

Strike, James. *Construction In Design.* Oxford: Butterworth-Heinemann Ltd., 1991.

Wilkinson, Chris. *Supersheds.* Oxford: Butterworth-Heinemann, Ltd., 1991.

Kjaergaard, Poul. *The Crystal Palace and Its Creation in 1851.* Copenhagen: The Art Academy's Architectural School, 1976.

Giedion, Siegfried. *Space, Time and Architecture,* 5th edition. Cambridge: Harvard University Press, 1967.

Frampton, Kenneth. *Modern Architecture: A Critical History,* 2nd edition. London: Thames and Hudson, 1985.

Norberg-Schulz, Christian. *Meaning in Western Architecture,* 2nd edition. London: Studio Vista, 1980.

Chemetov, Paul and Marrey, Bernard. *Architectures à Paris 1848–1914.* Paris: Dunod, 1984.

Orton, Andrew. *The Way We Build Now.* Workingham: Van Nostrand Reinhold, 1988.

Mainstone, Rowland. *Developments in Structural Form.* London: Allen Lane, 1975.

Vanggaard, Ole. *Dimensions.* Copenhagen: The Art Academy's Architecture School, 1992.

Cowan, Henry. *Architectural Structures,* 2nd edition. New York: Elsevier Publishing Company, 1976.

Architectural Review, December, 1989.

Byggekunst, No. 1/2. Oslo: 1991.

Davies, Colin. *British Pavilion, Seville Exposition 1992.* London: Phaidon Press, 1992.

Architectural Review, June, 1992.

Byggekunst, No. 4. Oslo: 1992.

Theme: Steel as Sculpture

Hilton, Tim. *On Caro's Later Work: Anthony Caro, Sculpture 1969-84.* An Arts Council Exhibition, 1984.

Fenton, Terry. *Anthony Caro.* London: Thames and Hudson, 1986.

Lyttleton, Celia. *European, 11–14.* "Iron, test of art in the marketplace." June, 1992.

Melville, Robert. *Architectural Review,* "Painting and Sculpture." December, 1963.

Ahronov, Ram, and Kent, Sarah. *Architectural Review,* "High Tech: Craft and Caro." July, 1984.

Daehlin, Erik. *Contemporary Norwegian Art.* Oslo: Technological Publishers Inc. 1990.

Serra, Richard. *Schriften Interviews 1970–1989.* Zurich: Benteli Publishers, 1990.

Krauss, Rosalind E. *Richard Serra/Sculpture.* New York: The Museum of Modern Art, 1986.

Lipman, Jean and Foote, Nancy. *Calder's Circus.* New York: E.P. Dutton/Whitney Museum of American Art, 1972.

Louisiana Review, No 5. "Alexander Calder."

Ribbed Structures

Architecture in Norway, Yearbook 1993. Oslo: Bonytt A/S and Norsk Arkitekturmuseum, 1993.

The Architectural Review, September, 1993.

Klein. Santiago *Calatrava: Bahnhof Stadelhofen, Zurich.* Stuttgart: Verlag Karl
Kramer, 1994.

Byggekunst, No. 5, 1994.

Theme: Steel Chairs

Le Corbusier: Oeuvre Complete 1929-34. Zurich: Verlag fur Architektur, 1957.

Schulze, Franz. *Mies van der Rohe.* Chicago: The University of Chicago Press, 1985.

Blaser, Werner. *Mies van der Rohe.* Zurich/Stuttgart: Verlag fur Architektur, 1965.

Page, Marian. *Furniture Designed by Architects.* New York: Whitney Library of
Design, 1980.

Christopher Wiik. *Marcel Breuer, Furniture and Interiors.* London: The
Architectural Press, 1981.

van Geest, Jan and Mácel, Otaker. *Stuhle aus Stahl.* Cologne: Verlag der
Buchhaundlung, Walther Konig, 1980.

Norberg-Schulz, Christian. *Casa Tugendhat, Brno.* Rome: Officina Edizione, 1984.

The Lunning Prize. Stockholm: National Museum, 1986.

Solaguren-Beascona, Felix. *Jacobsen.* Barcelona: Santa & Cole, 1991.

Multi-Bay Structures

Architectural Review, "Stansted Airport." May, 1991.

Architectural Monographs: Recent Works, No. 20. London: Foster Associates
Academy Editions, 1992.

Von Gerken, Marg & Partners: Large-Scale Projects. London: Academy Editions,
1992.

Norberg-Schulz, Christian. *Byggekunst,* No. 2. "A Masterpiece by Pier Luigi
Nervi." 1961

Smith, G.E. Kidder. *The New Architecture of Europe.* New York: Meridian Books,
The World Publishing Company, 1961.

Nervi, Pier Luigi. *Aesthetics and Technology in Buildings.* Cambridge: Harvard
University Press, 1965.

Lunde, Ivar and Lovseth, Morten. *Cross Section of a Moment* "Interpretation of
Place and Function." Oslo: College of Architecture, 1992.

Miles, Henry. *Architectural Review,* "Norse Accession." November, 1992.

Gronvold, Ulf. *Byggekunst,* No. 4, "Among the Trees of Knowledge." 1992

Theme: New Steel Design in Historic Buildings

Davey, Peter. *The Architectural Review,* "New Into Old." December, 1991.

Fjeld, Per Olaf. *Sverre Fehn, the Thought of Construction.* New York: Rizzoli, 1983.

Domus. *Galleria Nazionale del Palazzo della Pilotta, Parma.* May, 1987.

Steel In Combination With Other Materials

Gun Schonbeck. *St. Petri Church in Klippan: A Study of Sigurd Lewerentz's Architecture.* The Institute of Art & Science at Gothenburg University, 1985.

Aune, Petter. *Wood Structures, Part 1: Materials, Dimensions, Connections.* Trondheim: Tapir, 1992.

Moore, Rouan. *Blueprint Extra 04.* "Sackler Galleries Royal Academy." London: Wordsearch Ltd., 1991.

Viollet-le-Duc: *Lectures on Architecture,* 2 volumes. New York: Dover Publications, Inc., 1987.

Olav, Jan. *Byggekunst,* No. 5, "Truck Garage Ostfold Freight Center." 1989

Architectural Review, September, 1987.

Architectural Record, September, 1987.

L'Architecture aujourd'hui, December, 1987.

Lyall, Sutherland. *Architecture in Detail—Imagination Headquarters.* London: Phaidon Press Ltd., 1992.

Brookes, Alan and Grech, Chris. *Connection: Studies in Building Assembly.* Oxford: Butterworth Architecture, 1992.

Theme: Steel Details

Blake, Peter. *Mies van der Rohe.* Middlesex: Penguin Books, 1960.

Blaser, Werner. *Mies van der Rohe.* Zurich/Stuttgart: Artemis Verlag and Verlag fur Architektur, 1965.

Le Corbusier: Les Dernieres Oeuvres. Zurich: Les Editions d'Architecture Artemis, 1970.

Du Plateau Beaubourg au Centre Pompidou. Paris: Editions du Centre Pompidou, 1987.

Architectural Review, January, 1989.

Designers Journal, November, 1989.

Manser, Jose. *Joseph Shops, Eva Jiricna—Architecture in Detail.* London: Technology Press, 1991.

Norwegian Institute of Wood Technology. *Teknisk smaskrift,* No. 24. "Mechanical Means for Wood Connections." Oslo: 1991.

Blueprint Extra No. 04, "Sackler Galleries." London: Wordsearch Ltd., 1992.

9. Bridge Structures

Chemetov, Paul and Marrey, Bernard. *Architectures à Paris.* Paris: Dunod, 1984.

Hartung, Giselher. *The Iron Construction of the 19th Century.* Munich: Schirmer/Mosel, 1983.

Ostenfeld, Chr. *Motorway Bridge Across Lillebaelt.* Copenhagen: Chr. Ostenfeld & Jønson, 1970.

Leonhardt, Fritz. *Aesthetic and Gestalt.* London: The Architectural Press, 1982.

Billington, David, P. *The Tower and the Bridge.* Princeton: Princeton University Press, 1985.

DSB & the Road Directorate. *To Build a Bridge in Denmark,* exhibition catalog. Copenhagen: 1986.

Blaser, Werner. *Santiago Calatrava.* Basel/Boston/Berlin: Birkhaüser Publishers, 1989.

Slaich, Jörg and Bergermann, Rudolf. *Pedestrian Bridges,* exhibition catalogue. Zurich: 1992

Vegdirektoratet, Bruavdelingen. *Highway Commission Handbook—Bridge Design,* No. 164. Oslo: 1992.

Malet, Leo and Tardi. *Brouillard au Pont de Tolbiac.* Paris: Casterman, 1992.

Illustrations

246

INDEX